DATE DUE

Apr 25'80			
GAYLORD			PRINTED IN U.S.A.

THEOLOGY
OF THE KERYGMA

A Study in Primitive Preaching

PRENTICE-HALL INTERNATIONAL, INC.

London • *Tokyo* • *Sydney* • *Paris*

PRENTICE-HALL OF CANADA, LTD.

PRENTICE-HALL DE MEXICO, S.A.

THEOLOGY
OF THE KERYGMA

A Study in Primitive Preaching

CLAUDE H. THOMPSON

Emory University

PRENTICE-HALL, INC.
Englewood Cliffs, N. J.
1962

236
T37t

44014
Oct. 1962

TO SUE

Introduction

With the exception of the introductory first chapter, these studies have been presented as public addresses and the lecture style has been for the most part preserved. Chapters Two through Seven were delivered at Methodist Pastors' Schools in Virginia, Illinois, Missouri, and at a "Refresher School" at Gammon Theological Seminary in Atlanta, Georgia. Chapter Eight formed a part of a series of lectures given under the sponsorship of the Wesley Foundation at Memphis State University, and, after revision, at Methodist Pastors' Schools in Michigan, West Virginia, and Pennsylvania. Chapter One has been added to give historical perspective to the subject.

A word concerning the title is in order: While the term "kerygma" may seem somewhat technical, it has the advantage of coming from the New Testament. As indicated in Chapter One, it denotes the proclamation, the declaration, the heralding of the news of the redemptive deed of God in Christ as the core of Apostolic preaching. Since the term has come to be so widely used today, it has not seemed necessary to attempt to substitute a less technical English equivalent for it.

Biblical references, unless otherwise indicated in the text, have been taken from *The New Testament in Modern English*, by J. B. Phillips. The one-volume edition, published by The Macmillan Company, has been used.

A word of appreciation is expressed for the work of two typists, Mrs. Elizabeth Johnson and Mrs. Frances Stewart, who have labored faithfully to prepare the original and the final copies of the manuscript. Mr. Pat Chandler, graduate student in the Division of Religion at Emory University, has carefully checked each footnote and Biblical quotation.

Deepest gratitude is extended to my colleague, the Reverend Professor John Lawson of the Faculty of the Candler School of Theology, Emory University, for his painstaking care in reading each chapter. His penetrating insights and his frank and pointed suggestions have prevented needless blunders. And while he cannot, of course, be charged with any deficiencies which may have survived his critical evaluations, the study unmistakably bears the mark of his criticisms.

Finally, the writer is held by the conviction that sound theology and effective preaching are inseparable. Theologians can become so academic that intelligent laymen ignore them or lose patience. It is little less than sinful for the Christian Faith to be presented so obscurely as to fail to speak to the burning needs of men. And when preaching degenerates into citation of contemporary opinions, it has already betrayed the Faith once committed to the Saints. Whether this study succeeds in avoiding these two evils, the reader must decide. The writer can only claim to have tried.

CLAUDE H. THOMPSON

Emory University

Table of Contents

ix

ONE

Kerygmatic Theology

A significant event in Biblical studies occurred in 1936. C. H. Dodd then published three lectures, with an appendix: *The Apostolic Preaching and Its Developments*.[1] This brief volume is to be regarded as the source of what may be called "the theology of the kerygma." Seldom has a book of less than a hundred pages had such a wide influence. John Bright reminds us that to Dodd must go the credit for calling attention to this, "the most primary element in the New Testament."[2]

By now the theme of the *kerygma* is familiar to readers of modern theology. There seems to be an irreducible core of

---

[1] C. H. Dodd, *The Apostolic Preaching and Its Developments* (London: Hodder & Stoughton Limited, 1936).

[2] John Bright, *The Kingdom of God* (New York-Nashville: Abingdon Press, 1953), p. 189.

New Testament preaching which may neither be ignored nor diminished lest the Christian message be destroyed. Indeed, the total New Testament is but the elaboration and explication of this kerygma. Various scholars differ as to the precise elements which comprise it, but this central concern of the Gospel revolves around the life, mission, death, and resurrection of Jesus. This is the definitive structure in the light of which must be judged Christian ethics, church government, missions and evangelism, the history of the Christian enterprise, as well as preaching and every other activity of the church of God. Though at times the tendency arises to separate the expression of this message in words from the divine actions which give to the message its meaning, the two must never be divorced. What God in Christ *has done* gives authority to the proclamation; what is *proclaimed* points directly to these redemptive deeds. As Archibald M. Hunter has shown, the kerygma may indicate the act of proclamation or the thing proclaimed, that is, the *"content* of the *kerygma,"* "the coming of God's redemptive Rule in Jesus Christ." [3] Hunter thinks this latter meaning is more common in the New Testament. James M. Robinson believes that both ideas lie at the heart of the kerygma: "as the content of the message and as the act of preaching." [4]

It should be stated that, under the influence of existential thought, a third emphasis now becomes evident. Some define the kerygma as the proclamation of the past event in such a manner that it becomes a living present, "in which the past is contemporized." "Thus both as witness to past event and as experience of present event, the *kerygma* is central in primitive Christianity and contemporary theology." [5]

---

[3] Archibald M. Hunter, *The Message of the New Testament* (Philadelphia: The Westminster Press, 1944), pp. 24f.

[4] James M. Robinson, *A New Quest of the Historical Jesus,* Studies in Biblical Theology No. 25 (Naperville, Ill.: Alec R. Allenson, Inc., 1959), p. 41.

[5] *Ibid.,* pp. 42n, 43.

This kerygmatic theme seems firmly established as a clue to the unity of the New Testament. Hunter claims that *"the pattern of the kerygma runs right through the New Testament, giving to it, amid all its diversity, a deep essential unity."* [6] Robinson feels that the kerygma is "the center not only of the Gospels, but also of primitive Christianity itself." [7] It is said that Dodd's approach to the Bible "marked the first time that a single biblical concept was related to all New Testament material in a unified development." [8] And Otto Piper claims that Dodd "has succeeded in showing that notwithstanding the diversity of attitudes and theological principles of its authors, the NT bears witness to an underlying consensus concerning the subject matter and the meaning of its proclamation." [9]

THE THESIS

Since Dodd's thesis has such widespread influence, it should be stated. He finds in the kerygma six elements: (a) "The age of fulfilment has dawned." (b) "This has taken place through the ministry, death, and resurrection of Jesus." (c) "By virtue of the resurrection, Jesus has been exalted at the right hand of God, as Messianic head of the New Israel." (d) "The Holy Spirit in the Church is the sign of Christ's present power and glory." (e) "The Messianic Age will shortly reach its consummation in the return of Christ." * (f) "The kerygma always

---

[6] Archibald M. Hunter, *Introducing New Testament Theology* (Philadelphia: The Westminster Press, 1957), p. 68.

[7] Robinson, *op. cit.*, p. 38.

[8] Connolly Gamble, Jr., "The Literature of Biblical Theology: A Bibliographical Study," *Interpretation* (October, 1953), p. 471.

[9] Otto A. Piper, "The Origin of the Gospel Pattern," *Journal of Biblical Literature*, vol. lxxviii, part ii (June, 1959), p. 120.

* It is not at all *certain* that Jesus taught that He would return at an early date. It is quite possible that the Apostles did not fully understand Him, and made His eschatology more material and more immediate than He had intended.

closes with an appeal for repentance, the offer of forgiveness and of the Holy Spirit, and the promise of 'salvation.' " [10]

This interpretation of the kerygma is based, first of all, upon the Pauline Epistles. For example, in I Corinthians 1:23 and 2:2 is the reference to the "preaching" of Christ crucified. (The word "preaching" here is the English equivalent of kerygma, the term which is definitive for our study. Other examples follow.) This was the "foundation" given to the Apostle (I Corinthians 3:10f). One specific example is I Corinthians 15:3f where the death, burial, and resurrection are set forth. In Galatians 1:4 Christ is said to have given Himself for us "to rescue us from the present evil age," so that "those who believe belong no more to the present evil age, but to the glorious Age to Come." [11] Romans 10:8f speaks of the "burden of our preaching," "that Jesus Christ is the Lord and that God raised him from the dead." Additional Pauline citations include: Romans 1:2-5, 4:24f; II Corinthians 4:5; and possibly I Thessalonians 1:9-10.

Another important location of the kerygma motif is in the sermons in the Book of Acts, especially Peter's message on the Day of Pentecost (Acts 2:14-39); the speech at Solomon's Porch (Acts 3:12-26); the address before the Sanhedrin (Acts 4:8-12); and the speech to Cornelius (Acts 10:36-43). The same theme is also found in I Peter 1:10-12, 18f. As for the Gospels, Dodd regards the term itself as stated in Mark 1:1f, as "a virtual equivalent" for the kerygma.[12] In Matthew and Luke a further element is noted—that is the Davidic descent of Jesus which qualifies Him for Messianic mission.[13] As for the Fourth Gospel, the kerygma is no less clear than in the Synoptics, the Acts, and the Pauline Epistles. As Dodd says: "It is surely clear

---

[10] Dodd, *op. cit.*, pp. 21f.
[11] *Ibid.*, p. 11.
[12] *Ibid.*, p. 8.
[13] *Ibid.*, p. 52.

that the fourfold Gospel taken as a whole is an expression of the original apostolic Preaching." [14] He has also shown that this primitive kerygma is found in Hebrews as well as in other sections of the New Testament. A summary view may be cited from a scholar who owes much to Dodd's influence:

> Whatever the literary form may be—Gospel, History, Epistle, Apocalypse—and whoever the writer—Luke, Paul, John, the Writer to the Hebrews—the *kerygma* can be traced in the work. St. Mark's Gospel is expanded *kerygma,* as the *kerygma* controls the structure of the other three Gospels; its notes ring out clearly in the preaching of the first apostles; it throbs through the epistles of Paul and Peter and John; and it can be heard in the hieratic theology of Hebrews no less than in the apocalyptic drama of Revelation.[15]

PRO AND CON

Dodd was destined to provoke diverse judgments. But it should not be overlooked that he, too, had his predecessors. For example, as early as 1907 P. T. Forsyth was calling the Bible "a sermon, a κήρυγμα [kerygma], a preachment." [16] And a few years later he made it even more specific. Speaking of "a substantial dogmatic unity in the Gospel of the first Church," he says:

> There was, of course, no universal theological formula, there was not an orthodoxy; but certainly there was a common Apostolic Gospel, a κήρυγμα [kerygma] . . . And this theological κήρυγμα [kerygma] stands for us as the common chord in the three great names who represent the Apostolate—Peter, Paul, and John. It was a fixed but elastic tradition.[17]

---

14 *Ibid.,* p. 55.

15 Hunter, *op. cit.,* p. 68.

16 P. T. Forsyth, *Positive Preaching and the Modern Mind* (New York: A. C. Armstrong & Son, 1908), p. 10.

17 P. T. Forsyth, *The Principle of Authority* (London: Hodder and Stoughton, nd.), pp. 141f.

Martin Dibelius coined the formula "In the beginning was the sermon" ("Im Anfang war die Predigt") as early as 1919.[18] And Dodd himself has acknowledged a deep indebtedness to Rudolf Otto, especially for the understanding of the Kingdom which has come to be called "realized eschatology." We shall consider this aspect of Dodd's theology later, but this may be said at the moment: neither an exclusive future view of the Kingdom, nor one which regards it as "coming, very soon," that is in terms of a "thorough-going eschatology" (consequente Eschatologie) was adequate. Rather, Dodd is firm in asserting that the "most characteristic and distinctive of the Gospel sayings" affirm "the Kingdom of God to have come." These are "explicit and unequivocal." As he says: "The *eschaton* has moved from the future to the present, from the sphere of expectation into that of realized experience." [19]

The purpose of this reference is to show that the kerygmatic perspective was presented by Otto several years before Dodd's publication, and that Dodd received direction from Otto. Seldom does an author state this sort of influence so clearly:

> Among recent writers the one who does fullest justice to this idea is Rudolf Otto. His phrase for it is "der Schonanbruch des Reiches Gottes." I cannot see how anyone, after reading *Reich Gottes und Menschensohn,* pp. 51-73, could ever be content with interpretations which water down the meaning of these great sayings into a mere expectation that the Kingdom of God would come very soon.[20]

At any rate, while Dodd may be regarded as the popularizer of kerygmatic theology, at least in the English-speaking world, still he was profoundly influenced by others before him. Likewise, while some scholars have taken exception to what they

---

[18] See: Krister Stendahl, *The School of St. Matthew* (Uppsala: C. W. K. Gleerup, Lund, 1954), p. 13. See also: *Expository Times* (May, 1959), p. 232.
[19] C. H. Dodd, *The Parables of the Kingdom* (New York: Charles Scribner's Sons, 3rd edition, 1936), pp. 49f.
[20] *Ibid.,* p. 49n.

regard as an *exclusive* "realized eschatology" without regard to a future consummation, still the kerygmatic perspective which Dodd has set forth may be regarded at the present time as virtually established. For example, F. F. Bruce indicates that while the idea that the kingdom "has come" has been modified to include also the needed future emphasis, especially by W. G. Kümmel and Oscar Cullmann,[21] still "we can never go back on the achievements of Dodd and his school."[22]

Yet Dodd is not without his critics. Paul Schubert thinks the idea of "realized eschatology" is "too modern in conception to fit anyone in first century Palestine."[23] And Clarence Tucker Craig says that Dodd is "thrown into unnecessary contradictions by his theory of 'realized eschatology.'"[24] At the same time Craig approves the basic point of Dodd that the Gospel did not consist in mere memories of Jesus but in the saving facts of God's deliverance. This, as we maintain, is the center of Dodd's contribution. But even this has been challenged by Ernest W. Parsons. While he would agree with much of Dodd's study, "nevertheless, the main positions seem to be based upon too academic and too artificial a framework." He feels it might be desirable to seek for some underlying unity within the New Testament variety, yet Parsons desires to "move cautiously." Thus he doubts "that the thought movements of Christianity in the New Testament age can be interpreted by means of so rigid and simple a pattern as the author suggests." Dodd's work is regarded as "provocative," "challenging," even "frequently brilliant"; but "it leaves the reader not quite convinced."[25]

---

[21] F. F. Bruce, "Eschatology," *London Quarterly and Holborn Review* (April, 1958), p. 102.

[22] *Ibid.,* p. 103.

[23] Paul Schubert, "What Was Primitive Christianity?" (Book Review), *Christendom,* vol. ii, (1937), p. 494.

[24] Clarence Tucker Craig, "The Gospel of the Apostles" (Book Review), *Christian Century,* vol. 54 (1), (June 2, 1937), p. 715. Used by permission.

[25] Ernest W. Parsons (Book Review), *Journal of Religion,* vol. 18, (1938), pp. 91f. University of Chicago Press: "Copyright 1938 by the University of Chicago."

The controversy which Dodd precipitated pertains, in the main, to the exegesis of such passages as Mark 1:14f, Matthew 12:28, and Luke 11:20. This issue is whether the kingdom is to be understood as drawing near, at hand, or, as Dodd says: "The Kingdom of God has come." [26] James Y. Campbell claims that the interpretation must mean "has come near, is at hand"; that in the LXX there is "no good evidence that ἤγγικεν ever means 'has come.'" [27] Likewise, Kenneth Clark argues that "no linguistic evidence appears to support the contention that ἤγγικεν can mean 'has come,'" [28] And Cecil J. Cadoux asserts that Dodd's "elimination of futurist eschatology from the teaching of Jesus must undoubtedly be regarded as erroneous." [29] It is George Duncan's judgment that while Schweitzer had wrongly placed the kingdom entirely in the future, Dodd likewise carried his thesis too far in restricting it "to the living present." [30] R. H. Fuller feels that to place the decisive event of the kingdom in the past or in the present fails to do justice to the way in which Jesus' ministry is "keyed up to a future event," or, what is more serious, it "destroys the cruciality of the cross." [31] Kümmel contends that the idea of a present realized kingdom cannot be allowed since the scriptures under question must be translated as "the Kingdom of God has come near." [32] But one of the most emphatic rejections of Dodd comes from John J. Vincent. He regards the kerygmatic motif as "a convenient way of disposing of the theological difficul-

---

[26] Dodd, *Parables, op. cit.,* p. 44.

[27] James Y. Campbell, "The Kingdom of God Has Come," *Expository Times,* vol. 48 (November, 1936), pp. 91f.

[28] Kenneth W. Clark, "Realized Eschatology," *Journal of Biblical Literature,* lix (1940), p. 371.

[29] Cecil John Cadoux, *The Historic Mission of Jesus* (New York and London: Harper & Brothers, Lutterworth Press, nd.), p. 296n.

[30] George S. Duncan, *Jesus, Son of Man* (New York: The Macmillan Company, 1949), p. 190.

[31] R. H. Fuller, *The Mission and Achievement of Jesus,* Studies in Biblical Theology No. 12 (Chicago: Alec R. Allenson, Inc., 1934), pp. 48f.

[32] W. G. Kümmel, *Promise and Fulfilment,* Studies in Biblical Theology No. 23 (Naperville, Ill.: Alec R. Allenson, Inc., 1957), pp. 24f.

ties of the Synoptics." Possibly his criticism betrays a lack of thorough understanding of the discipline when he says: " 'Consistent kerygmatism' is a peculiarly Protestant malady, and may owe as much to the diminished Lutheran Doctrine of the Word as to the supposed contemporary need for a dehistoricised message." [33]

What may be said concerning this negative reaction to Dodd's thesis? Several conclusions seem relevant:

1. For the most part, *objections have been directed toward the idea of "realized eschatology" rather than toward the kerygmatic motif itself.* As Craig has said: "Many who read Dodd were more anxious to accept his realized eschatology than his stress upon the centrality of the Kerygma in the Christian proclamation." [34] Also as indicated above, Campbell, Clark, and Cadoux, as well as Fuller and Kümmel, concentrate their criticism on the rejection of a future eschatology.

It should not be overlooked that some of those who reject Dodd's interpretation of the kingdom as present in favor of the doctrine that it "has drawn near," still concur in the view that the present reality of the kingdom must be affirmed. Thus, Robinson says:

> For even though we must understand ἤγγικεν to mean 'has drawn near' rather than 'has come,' it still refers to something having taken place: the times have shifted, the kingdom is now near because it has moved from a vague distance to a near position, a shift which has already taken place.[35]

2. *Critics have been prone to attack this one aspect of Dodd's thought and overlook his own inclusion of a future*

---

[33] John J. Vincent, "Didactic Kerygma in the Synoptic Gospels," *Scottish Journal of Theology,* vol. 10 (1957), p. 263n.

[34] Clarence Tucker Craig, "The Apostolic Kerygma in the Christian Message," *Journal of Bible and Religion,* vol. 20 (1952), p. 183.

[35] James M. Robinson, *The Problem of History in Mark,* Studies in Biblical Theology No. 21 (Naperville, Ill.: Alec R. Allenson, Inc., 1957), p. 24.

consummation to the kingdom. For example, even in his early volume, he speaks of this consummation:

> While, however, the New Testament affirms with full seriousness that the great divine event has happened, there remains a residue of eschatology which is not exhausted in the 'realized eschatology' of the Gospel, namely, the element of sheer finality.... Thus the idea of a second coming of Christ appears along with the emphatic assertion that His coming in history satisfies all the conditions of the eschatological event, *except* that of absolute finality.[36]

It is likely that this insight has led Frederick C. Grant, while not totally committed to Dodd's thesis, to defend him against misunderstanding. He thinks that Dodd's term, "realized eschatology," is "gravely misunderstood." "Clearly he never meant that Jesus thought that his own times already belonged under the fully realized Kingdom of God." Indeed the death of John the Baptist, the massacre of pilgrims at Jerusalem, and the threat of further divine judgments made it clear "that the Age to Come was not already here. *But it had drawn near.*" "The Kingdom was so near at hand that one could truly describe it as really present." [37]

3. *Dodd has sought to clarify his own views, even to modify them to include the idea of the kingdom yet to come.* One example will be sufficient. In 1951 he published some broadcast talks under the title, *The Coming of Christ.* He refers to the entrance of Christ into history as "something quite new . . . from beyond the frontier of human existence, and the whole outlook for mankind in this world was permanently altered." Thus,

---

36 Dodd, *Apostolic Preaching, op. cit.,* p. 93.

37 Frederick C. Grant, "Biblical Studies: Views and Reviews," *Theology Today,* vol. 14 (April, 1957), p. 50. (Printed with permission of *Theology Today.*)

. . . what came to earth then was final and decisive for the whole meaning and purpose of human existence, and we shall meet it again when history has been wound up. . . . At the last frontier-post we shall encounter God in Christ.[38]

Indeed, Dodd is quite specific in saying that Jesus sought to prepare "His disciples for a time of troubles . . . Consequently He must have contemplated a further period of history after His departure." [39] But during this further period, while the disciples were to be constantly persuaded that "His total career on earth was the crisis in which the long awaited kingdom of God came upon men," there was another dimension to this Advent hope. Dodd speaks for himself on this:

There are some mysterious sayings about the coming of the Son of Man which I have passed over too lightly. There are passages where we are told that before He comes there will be a breakdown of the physical universe. I said before that it would be absurd to take literally the language about the darkened sun and falling stars. All the same, we cannot easily dismiss the impression that the final scene is laid where the world of space, time and matter is no longer in the picture. It is in no world of time and space that the nations of the dead, as well as the living, stand before Christ for judgment, as we are told they will. And there is that strange thing that Jesus is reported to have said at His trial before the High Priest: "You shall see the Son of Man seated at the right hand of the Almighty." Make all allowance we may for symbolic language, can we give any meaning to such a statement unless we think of another world than this? . . . Surely the total impression is that the forecasts of a coming of Christ in history (fulfilled in His resurrection) are balanced by forecasts of a coming beyond history: definitely, I should say, *beyond* history, and not as a further event *in* history, not even the last event.[40]

---

[38] C. H. Dodd, *The Coming of Christ*, (London and New York: Cambridge University Press, 1951), p. 38.

[39] *Ibid.*, p. 19.

[40] *Ibid.*, pp. 16f.

It is when considering the "final drop of the curtain," death, that Dodd argues for a boundary which is not just a dead end. Rather is the Almighty God who decrees this boundary the God who "meets us at the frontier: where the life of our race reaches its term: God in Christ." At this boundary reference to the final coming of the Son of Man makes sense.

Unlike His first coming, it is not an event *in* history. It is the point at which *all* history is taken up into the larger whole of God's eternal purpose.[41]

We speak of this as His *second* coming. But this reminds us that there was a *first*. "At that one point, God in Christ made Himself into a character in history." [42] Coming within our boundaries and accepting our limitations, He illumined the values which history is meant to exhibit. In this encounter with "political ambition, mistaken religious zeal, personal and class prejudice, and the like," He put Himself under death and destruction as the way to victory over them. Thus we live at the center of what history means—as interpreted by His triumph over these enemies. Therefore, the Second Coming is seen in the culmination of the meaning of His first coming, that is, His ideal for human life—individual and corporate— the path we must travel to achieve it, the final relation between "man and his Maker," and "the true nature of the last frontier-post, and who it is that awaits us there. More than that we do not need to know." [43]

It seems, therefore, in the light of Dodd's purpose to clarify or modify his views, that he has two things in mind. He wishes to resist an optimistic idea of inevitable progress in history, and to avoid speculations which, obviously, are quite beyond

---

41 *Ibid.,* p. 27.
42 *Ibid.,* p. 27.
43 *Ibid.,* p. 32.

the ability of our minds to grasp in this life. At the same time, he is sure that any futurist interpretation of the kingdom must be in harmony with what we know of its inauguration in terms of "realized eschatology." It is important, in this connection, to note that Dodd has indicated his willingness to use another term: "sich realisierende Eschatologie," freely—"eschatology in the process of realization," though Dodd claims he is unable to translate it into English.[44] This concession should satisfy Dodd's most severe critics.

4. *Significant scholars support Dodd's thesis that the kingdom "has come."* [45] The late R. H. Lightfoot regards the likely translation as "the time of fulfilment has come, the Kingdom of God has appeared." [46] Duncan is persuaded that the tendency to think of Jesus as merely the herald of a coming kingdom is inadequate. It is not unreasonable to hold "that the Kingdom has indeed dawned; it has come so near as to be a present reality." [47] The same view is expressed by Hunter: "What is the sense of saying that 'the appointed time has fully come' if in fact the Kingdom is still round the corner?" [48] Paul Minear prefers Dodd's realized eschatology to the futurist conception claiming that the "Christians recognize the new *kairos* as *a present stage of fulfilment*. The *kairos* has been fulfilled." (Mark 1:15) [49] A similar view is expressed in his book, *Eyes of Faith*.[50]

5. *"Realized eschatology" may be extended to cover the*

---

[44] Joachim Jeremias, *The Parables of Jesus*, Translated by S. H. Hooke (New York: Charles Scribner's Sons, 1955), p. 159.

[45] W. R. Hutton, "The Kingdom of God Has Come," *Expository Times*, vol. 64 (December, 1952), p. 91.

[46] R. H. Lightfoot, *History and Interpretation in the Gospel* (New York: Harper & Brothers Publishers, nd.), p. 107nl.

[47] Duncan, *op. cit.*, p. 41.

[48] Hunter, *Introducing New Testament Theology, op. cit.*, p. 27.

[49] Paul S. Minear, "Time and the Kingdom," *Journal of Religion*, vol. 24 (April, 1944), pp. 83, 86. University of Chicago Press: "Copyright 1944 by the University of Chicago."

[50] Paul S. Minear, *Eyes of Faith* (Philadelphia: The Westminster Press, 1946), pp. 88f.

future. Many scholars who do not completely endorse Dodd's view still admit the validity of the interpretation of the kingdom as a present reality. For example, Cadoux, surveying the debate between Campbell, Clark, Dodd, and others, concludes that the kingdom "has drawn near." [51] Vincent Taylor feels that Dodd overstates the idea that the kingdom "has come," and he prefers the translation "is at hand" or "has drawn near." Then he shows that "the difference, of course, is not great, since only a negligible interval is meant, and there is clear evidence that Jesus believed the *Basileia* to be present in Himself and His ministry." [52]

Again, while Kümmel rejects Dodd's limitation of the idea of the kingdom as only "realized," he still holds that it was Jesus' conviction "that the future Kingdom of God had already begun in his activity." Furthermore, as Kümmel clearly states: "It is the meaning of the mission of Jesus, when announcing the *approach* of the Kingdom of God, to make this future at the same time already now a present reality." Or again: "It is quite firmly established that the eschatological consummation, the Kingdom of God, has already become a present reality in the ministry of Jesus." And to show how Kümmel gathers up Dodd's idea within his own, this reference may be used: "Here too the message of the approaching Kingdom of God is actually illuminated by the knowledge that through Jesus' activities *the future consummation is brought into the present.*" [53]

Cullmann, admitting his indebtedness to Kümmel, expresses a similar view. The kingdom has, "in fact, drawn nearer with Christ." "With him we have entered into the final period of time in the present world. . . . We are in the final phase of the period, the duration of which we do not know. . . .

---

[51] Cadoux, *op. cit.*, p. 198n4.

[52] Vincent Taylor, *The Gospel According to Mark* (London and New York: Macmillan & Co., Ltd., St. Martin's Press, Inc., 1952), p. 167.

[53] Kümmel, *op. cit.*, pp. 107f, 109, 114. [Italics mine]

According to Jesus himself, his death is the decisive event which ushers in the coming of the kingdom." "We are living in the last age of time. This last age is a fragment of the future, the only part of the coming age which exists in the present age." [54] Thus, Cullmann has framed for us the figures of speech, "D-Day," as God's decisive intervention in the warfare with evil in the redemptive deeds of Christ, and "V-Day," the *parousia*, "The hope of the final victory is so much the more vivid because of the unshakably firm conviction that the battle that decides the victory has already taken place." [55]

Others who hold this synthesis of the present realized kingdom and a future consummation include Eric Rust, who regards the *eschaton*, "the end of history," as already present in Jesus Christ. He holds that "time has already been filled with eternity," yet the "hiddenness" of it implies "a final consummation when the full glory shall shine forth." [56] Bruce says with the death and resurrection of Christ "eschatology has indeed been inaugurated" but this inauguration "points on to consummation." [57] Duncan feels that both "futurist eschatology" and "realized eschatology" need each other "as a complement if the progress and consummation of God's Kingdom are to be seen in true perspective." [58] Thomas E. McCollough likewise prefers Dodd's view to that of Schweitzer since it at least avoids the position that Jesus was mistaken in His eschatological expectations. Yet he feels that Dodd errs "in his radical devaluation of history in relegating the significance of the Kingdom wholly to the transcendent sphere." Thus Dodd's emphasis "tends to be idea-centered, instead of Christ-centered," and the

---

[54] Oscar Cullmann, *The Early Church*, Edited by A. J. B. Higgins (Philadelphia: The Westminster Press, 1956), pp. 153-155.

[55] Oscar Cullmann, *Christ and Time* (Philadelphia: The Westminster Press, 1950), pp. 84, 87.

[56] Eric Rust, "Time and Eternity in Biblical Thought," *Theology Today* (October, 1953), p. 349. (Printed with permission of *Theology Today*.)

[57] Bruce, *op. cit.*, p. 103.

[58] Duncan, *op. cit.*, p. 190.

element of demythologizing on his construction reduces the content of the kingdom "to a bare existentialism." Hence there must be added to Dodd's contention that the purpose of history has been fully realized in Christ, the declaration of the "ultimate unveiling of the victorious Christ." Realized eschatology does not do justice to God's teleological control of history, nor to the nature of the New Testament hope. Dodd's theory is open to criticism "on the basis of what it denies; its great value lies in what it affirms," that is, "life in the Kingdom of God is a present reality." [59] Finally, William Manson has put the matter cryptically: "There is a realized eschatology. There is also an eschatology of the unrealized. . . . What *is* realized in Christ in the present era is the character of the *Eschaton*, not its complete substance. . . . Christianity, therefore, from the beginning exhibits an essential bi-polarity. The End has come! The End has not come!" [60]

What is our conclusion of this survey? It may be stated simply: So much attention has been given to Dodd's idea of "realized eschatology" that the importance of his basic theme could be overlooked. While others have corrected his partial view, still his introduction of the definitive place of the kerygmatic approach to the Gospel has been repeatedly validated.

William Baird's attempt to bring into dynamic harmony the views of Dodd and Bultmann is worthy of notice. Dodd, in Baird's interpretation, finds the early Christian message in "a formula of facts and doctrines about God's action in Christ," whereas Bultmann understands the Gospel as "God's powerful act in which Christ is dynamically present calling men to a decision of faith." [61] Baird is correct in showing that there need not be a contradiction since Dodd finds the message

---

[59] Thomas E. McCollough, "Realized Eschatology and C. H. Dodd," *Religion in Life*, vol. 26 (Summer, 1957), pp. 431-435.

[60] William Manson, "Eschatology in the New Testament," *Scottish Journal of Theology Occasional Papers No. 2*, Oliver & Boyd (1953), p. 7.

[61] William Baird, "What is the Kerygma? A Study of I Cor. 15:3-8 and Gal. 1:11-17," *Journal of Biblical Literature*, lxxvi (September, 1957), p. 183.

located within "an eschatological setting which gives significance to the facts," and Bultmann recognizes that the kerygma "may also be formulated in a series of abstract propositions." [62] Baird's conclusion is that Dodd and Bultmann correct each other: Dodd reminds us that the Gospel may not be "de-historicized," since history is important for the Gospel; Bultmann reminds us that the Gospel may not be turned into a dogma since it is important for faith.[63]

KERYGMA, HISTORY, AND MYTH

The reference to Bultmann raises the question of the relation between kerygma, history, and myth in the proclamation of the Gospel. This is too complex a problem to enter into here adequately, but three things may be said:

1. Insofar as Bultmann's "demythologizing" would cut the Christian faith free from its historical rootage, it must be rejected. This has been clearly argued by Fuller, who demonstrates that the kerygma of the church "is not an arbitrary interpretation imposed upon an arbitrarily selected stretch of history, but that it has an intelligible basis in that history." [64] With vigor, and a touch of impatient, Robert E. Cushman has used the criticisms of Bultmann by Julius Schniewind [65] to unveil the unnecessary historical skepticism shown by Bultmann. Cushman finds greater continuity between the "kerygma and the impelling occasion, the originative event" in history, than Bultmann allows. He suggests that could Bultmann only take seriously this original and necessary historical rootage of the Gospel, "there would then be the basis for

---

[62] William Baird, "What is the Kerygma? A Study of I Cor. 15:3-8 and Gal. 1:11-17," *Journal of Biblical Literature*, lxxvi (September, 1957), p. 183.

[63] *Ibid.*, p. 191.

[64] Fuller, *op. cit.*, p. 117.

[65] Julius Schniewind, *Kerygma and Myth*, Edited by Hans Werner Bartsch, Translated by Reginald H. Fuller (London: SPCK, 1953), pp. 45f.

modifying the nearly complete discontinuity between Jesus and 'the Christ.' "

> There would be the possibility of giving the Christ-event a habitation and a home somewhat less transcendent than the dimension of Geschichte. In such a case, it might be feasible once more to consider the possibility that an 'act of God' could occur in God's own world. In that event even the Incarnation might again receive serious consideration. Until then it is clear that, for Bultmann, it remains a splendid symbol of the universal possibility of passage from fallen existence to authentic being through the cruciform moment of decision.[66]

For Dodd, the kerygma is far more firmly rooted in history than it is for Bultmann.

2. One of Bultmann's own students has carefully shown how a post-Bultmannian "school" is now turning toward "A New Quest of the Historical Jesus." [67] Indeed, Robinson indicates that there is implicit in Bultmann's own position the elements needed for this quest. Ernst Käsemann has argued that there is available authentic historical material regarding the life of our Lord, and that this must be taken seriously as evidence, lest we "find ourselves committed to a mythological Lord." Fuchs has argued that Jesus' message was dependent upon His action. Thus the disciples saw His death as a divine action which was for the primitive church exhibited in the sacraments and embodied in the kerygma. Günther Bornkamm argues that the Easter event constituted the inbreaking of the new world of God into the old world of sin and death. Thus Jesus' eschatological message, including His own life and death, "has been continued in christological terms by the Easter faith and the Christian *kerygma*." [68] Likewise, Robinson, who has

---

[66] Robert Cushman, "Is the Incarnation a Symbol?" *Theology Today* (July, 1958), pp. 181f. (Printed with permission of *Theology Today*.)

[67] Robinson, *New Quest, op. cit.*, see pp. 12f, 16f.

[68] *Ibid.*, p. 18.

written in English on these matters, finds "the procedure of a New Quest" based upon a methodology beyond that of historical positivism. Nor can a reconstruction of Jesus' teachings establish the validity of Christianity. "We recognize as basic, that historiography cannot and should not prove a *kerygma* which proclaims Jesus as *eschatological* event calling for *existential* commitment." [69] Rather, Robinson argues that Jesus himself proclaimed the kerygma, that he claimed exalted titles for Himself and predicted his death and resurrection.[70] While Jesus did not himself teach a Christology, His call to decision implies a Christology.[71] Furthermore, the eschatological message of Jesus and the kerygmatic Christology of the church, while different in terminology, have the same rootage in fact. Thus, "It is this existential meaning latent in Jesus' message which is constitutive of his selfhood, expresses itself in his action, and is finally codified in the Church's *kerygma*." [72] Robinson's conclusion goes far to obviate the defects of Bultmann: "The selfhood of Jesus is equally available to us—apparently both *via* historical research and *via* the *kerygma*—as a possible understanding of our existence." [73]

This insistence upon the inseparability of the kerygma and history has been borne out by other scholars. For example, Gogarten denies that the "person of Jesus and His history have been replaced by a *kerygma* which is entirely devoid of history and which is moreover only a more or less arbitrary product of the earliest Christian Church." [74] The kerygma is not simply a report of something that has happened, for "after all a reporter is not a herald." Rather it is the fact that God sent Jesus into the world, and that the content of His message

---

[69] *Ibid.,* p. 94.
[70] *Ibid.,* pp. 100f.
[71] *Ibid.,* p. 111.
[72] *Ibid.,* p. 123.
[73] *Ibid.,* p. 125.
[74] Frederick Gogarten, *Demythologizing and History* (London: SCM Press, Ltd., 1955), p. 75.

"is the salvation which God has prepared for mankind," and "this salvation is God Himself, in His turning Himself as God towards mankind, as He does precisely in this proclamation of Jesus." [75] Likewise, Bo Reicke speaks of the earliest Christian preaching given in Acts as formed on a common pattern "soon after the resurrection of Christ." [76] Yet the historical ground of this preaching "must principally have depended upon the personal teaching of Jesus." [77] Taylor here agrees: "It is undoubtedly true that Mark's Gospel reflects the ideas of the primitive Christian *Kerygma,* but it does this because the earliest preaching rested upon what Jesus had done and taught." [78]

No one has contended more vigorously for the relation of preaching and history than Jeremias. He argues that every verse of the Gospels tells us that the origin of Christianity is not the kerygma, not the resurrection experience of the disciples, not the Christ idea, "but an historical event, to wit, the appearance of the Man Jesus of Nazareth, who was crucified under Pontius Pilate, and His message." [79] The kerygma proclaims an historical event, namely, "God in Christ" who "died for our sins according to the Scriptures." This is the very heart of the kerygma.[80] The Jesus of history was the content of His message. The kerygma always refers back of itself to Him. The Good News of Jesus and the proclamation of the Early Church were inseparable. "He who isolates the message of Jesus ends up in Ebionitism. He who isolates the Kerygma of the Early Church ends up in Docetism." [81]

But this inseparability of history and the kerygma has a

---

[75] *Ibid.,* p. 69.

[76] Anton Fridrichsen, *et al., The Root of the Vine* (London: Dacre Press, A. & C. Black, Ltd., 1953), p. 129.

[77] *Ibid.,* p. 129.

[78] Taylor, *Mark, op. cit.,* pp. 133f.

[79] Joachim Jeremias, "The Present Position in the Controversy Concerning the Problem of the Historical Jesus," *Expository Times,* lxix (1958), p. 336.

[80] *Ibid.,* p. 336.

[81] *Ibid.,* p. 339.

further dimension: namely, "a frame of reference . . . which would convey unity to the constitutive elements of the kerygma." [82] This was embodied in what Piper calls the *homologia*, that is to say, the confession that "Jesus is the Christ" or "Jesus is the Lord." [83] The common Gospel pattern throughout the primitive Church declared that the Jesus who was proclaimed as Christ or Lord was the Jesus who "had manifested his messiahship in and through his public ministry." [84] There was a revelation which came through the public ministry of Jesus and which the disciples apprehended. This demonstrates that "the gospel story had supernatural kerygmatic authority." [85] Thus the order would be: *divine redemptive activity—seen in the ministry of Jesus as Messiah—apprehended by those who witnessed His life, death, resurrection—confessed as Lord (Kyrios) having supernatural authority—embodied in the corporate life of the ecclesia—and recorded in the Holy Scriptures.* There is here, therefore, the convergence of the eschatological intervention of God in history, and the church's recognition of this event in Christological proclamation. The two unite to form the core of primitive preaching, the kerygma.

SIGNIFICANCE OF THE THESIS

It is hardly surprising that the writer who pioneered the notion of the kerygma should be important for the theology of the kerygma. Craig refers to the movement from the liberalism of Harnack and Troeltsch to the kerygmatic perspective of Dodd. "It was the merit of a thin little volume by C. H. Dodd on *The Apostolic Preaching and Its Developments* to bring this issue forcibly before the Anglo-Saxon religious

---

[82] Piper, *op. cit.,* p. 121.
[83] *Ibid.,* p. 121.
[84] *Ibid.,* p. 123.
[85] *Ibid.,* p. 124.

world." [86] Hunter regards this volume as "one of the most important and positive contributions to New Testament science in our generation." [87] Floyd V. Filson has referred to Dodd's study as "one of the most significant books of the last generation in the field of New Testament study." [88] Dodd is given credit by R. R. Williams for bequeathing the meaning of the Greek term to the English world, and showing how similar it is to the Apostles Creed.[89] Finally, G. Ernest Wright speaks of the kerygma as "the nerve center of the New Testament, of which the Gospels are expansions." [90]

The subsequent chapters of our study will attempt to outline the theological implications for our time of the kerygma. There seems to be a valid place for a theological approach to this, the irreducible core of primitive Christian preaching.

---

[86] Craig, *Journal of Bible and Religion*, vol. 20, *op. cit.*, pp. 182f.

[87] Hunter, *The Message of the New Testament*, *op. cit.*, p. 26.

[88] Floyd V. Filson, *Jesus Christ the Risen Lord* (New York-Nashville: Abingdon Press, 1956), p. 33.

[89] R. R. Williams, *The Acts of the Apostles* (New York: The Macmillan Company, 1953), pp. 47f.

[90] G. Ernest Wright, "Wherein Lies the Unity of the Bible?" *Journal of Bible and Religion*, vol. 20 (1952), p. 197.

TWO

The Isness
Of The Shall Be!

A contemporary theologian has used the expression, "the *isness* of the *was*." He was seeking to show that the significance of Christ cannot be confined to the first third of the first century. Indeed, His significance for the twentieth century is in no sense inferior to His significance for the first century. In an authentic sense He is the "contemporary Christ," even the "cosmic Christ," for any century; since it is He who, by holding together the "beginning" and the "end" of all time, gives meaning to every age. This the writer of the Apocalypse saw when he described Him as "the Alpha and Omega, the beginning and the end." (Revelation 21:6)

However, the accent of kerygmatic theology is slightly different. It is "the *isness* of the *shall be*." The new age has come. "The age of fulfilment has dawned." [1] Through the

---

[1] Dodd, *Apostolic Preaching, op. cit.,* p. 38.

Incarnation of God in Jesus Christ the hopes of the Day of the Lord had become a reality. "This is something which was predicted by the prophet Joel." (Acts 2:16) "God had foretold through all His prophets that His Christ must suffer and this was how His words came true." (Acts 3:18) "All the prophets from Samuel onwards who have spoken at all have foretold these days." (Acts 3:24) Or, as in Mark 1:15: "The time has come at last—the Kingdom of God has arrived."

The long wait for the time of the Messiah had ended. God had entered history to give it a new dimension and a new direction.

> Hail to the Lord's Anointed,
> Great David's Greater Son!
> Hail, in the time appointed,
> *His reign on earth begun!* [2]

To express this idea of the present reality of the kingdom, Dodd speaks of "realized eschatology." [3] Many scholars, while deviating from him on details, concur that in the Advent of Christ, God acted to establish the kingdom. For example, Bright claims that the future tense of the Old Testament had now become an emphatic present, "a present indicative—the Kingdom is *here!*" [4] Hunter shows that the kingdom is not some moral disposition in men's hearts, much less an ideal utopia constructed through human efforts, but the intervention of the Living God "breaking decisively into history in judgment and blessing," "no longer a shining hope on the far horizon but a *fait accompli.*" [5] Harold Roberts asserts that

[2] James Montgomery, *The Methodist Hymnal,* #85. [Italics mine]

[3] Dodd, *Apostolic Preaching, op. cit.,* pp. 85, 233; *The Parables of the Kingdom, op. cit.,* p. 51.

[4] Bright, *The Kingdom of God, op. cit.,* pp. 197, 216.

[5] A. M. Hunter, *A Pattern for Life* (Philadelphia: The Westminster Press, 1953), p. 69; *The Work and Words of Jesus* (Philadelphia: The Westminster Press, 1951), p. 72.

"the early Christians were persuaded that they were living in the age of fulfilment." [6] Filson shows that in the work of the crucified and risen Christ, "the fulfilment had *already begun.*" [7] Amos N. Wilder argues that Jesus was proclaiming a "sublime Tomorrow" as already dawning for His generation as a new creation of God.[8] Bultmann, whose eschatological views deviate from those of Dodd, finds in Jesus "the eschatological event." [9] He is the "eschatological salvation-bringer," his coming *"is the eschatological event."* [10] We see in Him "the action of God by which God has set an end to the old world." [11] Thus Jesus says in the proclamation of the kingdom: *"Now the time is come! God's Reign is breaking in! The end is here!"* [12]

What, then, do we mean by the present reality of the kingdom? Alfred North Whitehead once said: "Christ gave His life. It is for Christians to discern the doctrine." [13] We may say: *Christ inaugurated the kingdom. It is for Christians to clarify the meaning.* We are concerned now with the meaning of the divine deed, the Christ-Event, that to which the kerygma brought witness.

---

[6] Harold Roberts, *Jesus and the Kingdom of God* (London: The Epworth Press, 1955), pp. 102, 29f.

[7] Filson, *Jesus Christ the Risen Lord, op. cit.,* p. 43.

[8] Amos N. Wilder, *New Testament Faith for Today* (New York: Harper & Brothers, 1955), p. 85.

[9] Rudolf Bultmann, *Jesus Christ and Mythology* (New York: Charles Scribner's Sons, 1958), p. 80.

[10] Rudolf Bultmann, *Theology of the New Testament,* vol. ii, Translated by Kendrick Grobel (New York: Charles Scribner's Sons, 1955), p. 37.

[11] Rudolf Bultmann, *History and Eschatology* (Edinburgh: The University Press, 1957), p. 151.

[12] Rudolf Bultmann, *Theology of the New Testament,* vol. i (New York: Charles Scribner's Sons, 1951), p. 6.

[13] A. N. Whitehead, *Religion in the Making* (New York: The Macmillan Company, 1926), p. 56.

FINAL JUDGMENT IS—NOW:

For one thing, to claim that the kingdom has already come means that the Last Judgment is *now*. John Wesley's famous sermon, "The Great Assize," declared that

> The Son of Man shall bow the sky,
> All nations in that day shall meet,
> Arraign'd at His tremendous bar
> Behold Him on His judgment seat.[14]

This Assize was pictured as a colossal courtroom where all persons—past, present, and future—were to be gathered into one vast and solemn assembly. The notion that the human race stands before the judgment of God, and that it is well possible for sinful man to be visited with sudden destruction, is a thought all too familiar to this insecure generation, as it goes in fear of its own handiwork.

But the trouble with Mr. Wesley's Great Assize was that it was too far away. Whatever a future judgment may mean after a blasted earth, a millenium hence, it strikes little dread into me, now. But I can understand judgment here and now—in my street, in my town, on my campus, in my church, in my home, within my own soul.

The event of Christ *is* the final judgment. Nothing can be more final. "This *is* the judgment—that light has entered the world and men have preferred darkness to light because their deeds are evil." (John 3:19) The idea of a future, final judgment need not be denied in order to assert the present certainty of that finality. The difficult passage of Hebrews 10:26f, which warns against deliberate apostasy, reminds us

---

[14] John Wesley, *The Poetical Works of John and Charles Wesley*, collected and arranged by G. Osborn, D.D. (1871), vol. x, p. 392.

that "there can be no further sacrifice for sin for us but only a terrifying expectation of judgment and the fire of God's indignation." But notice: the judgment which "will one day consume all that sets itself against Him" has already been set within the bounds of history! Theo Preiss has correctly seen that eschatology "like everything else is severely concentrated on Christology." "In the Son of Man, the future Judge, judgment is already mysteriously present." [15] As John Whale would remind us, we are as near the Fall as was Moses,[16] so we may assert that we live as near the Empty Tomb as did Paul and Simon Peter. The test of the Living Presence of Christ is whether His Risen Self is as real to us as it was to those two men in the Emmaus home. Or as St. Paul could say: "Last of all, as if to one born abnormally late, He appeared to me!" (I Corinthians 15:8)

Thus my friend, in his campus jargon, calls this "the isness of the was"! Let it be remembered there is also the "isness of the shall be!" We not only are contemporaries of what has been. We daily participate in what shall be. We are living in the *eschaton*, "The Last Times," as the Bible calls them. We are alive in the last days. The coming of Christ introduced a new dimension into history, a dimension of judgment, of *krisis*, that sort of judgment which carries all the marks of finality except that of sheer consummation. As Herbert Butterfield has reminded us: "Every instant is 'eschatological,' or, as one person has put it, like the point in the fairy-story where the clock is just about to strike twelve." [17]

Over and over again we meet this idea of the krisis in the "now time" of the New Testament. "Now is the time for the judgment of this world to begin, and now will the spirit that

---

[15] Theo Preiss, *Life in Christ*, translated by Harold Knight; Studies in Biblical Theology, No. 13 (Naperville, Ill.: Alec R. Allenson, Inc., 1954, 1957), p. 18.

[16] J. S. Whale, *Christian Doctrine* (New York: The Macmillan Company, 1945), p. 52.

[17] Herbert Butterfield, *Christianity and History* (New York: Charles Scribner's Sons, 1950), p. 121.

rules this world be driven out." (John 12:31) "When the proper time came, God sent His Son—." (Galatians 4:4) "But if I with the finger of God cast out devils, no doubt the kingdom of God is come upon you." (Luke 11:20, KJV) Thus we "have tasted the good word of God, and the powers of the world to come." (Hebrews 6:5, KJV)

This means that I live every moment within the boundary of the judgment, of krisis. Every hour is an hour of destiny. Every moment of life is fraught with eternal significance, every moment under the final judgment of God. Nothing can be more final than to know that I live daily under the scrutiny of the risen Christ. This means that in all life's so-called ordinary duties I stand at the "judgment seat of Christ." As Theo Preiss has so forcefully put it:

> This moment becomes invested with infinite seriousness not only because the time is short and the Parousia is near but because it is loaded with the infinite weight of the mysterious presence in our neighbour of the Son of Man and of God himself.... Man is confronted by his heavenly judge whenever he sees the need of his neighbour, the judgment and the *final destiny of each one is in reality decided at the present moment*.[18]

Why does Preiss write in this manner? Because, in the final analysis, the only moment we ever possess is this final moment, the one in which we now live—or die! Thus,

> The only moments which henceforth have positive value and are really historical are those which are filled with humble gestures of love and service. For such moments are already secretly pregnant with eternity.[19]

Nearly half a century ago, almost unrecognized, Forsyth saw this truth of the judgment in Christ:

---

18 Preiss, *op. cit.*, p. 59. [Italics mine]
19 *Ibid.*, p. 59.

> The Cross of Christ is God's last judgment on all sin. . . . It is the last resource of the Almighty Holiness; and *His* last resource is the end of all things—which is now always at hand in a kingdom both coming and come.[20]

A task of Christian ministers is to restore to the eleven o'clock hour of worship a sense of the present mighty judgment of God, until that same sense of destiny which stirred the soul of timid folk in early Christian days comes to grip the church today. Wherever these early folk went they were possessed by the certainty that nothing could possibly happen in the future which could be essentially different from what had already happened to them. It could only be more of what had already taken place. They knew they were living "between the times," within the final judgment.

LIFE AS INVOLVEMENT

Since final judgment is ever with us, life must be seen as confronted by the issues of that judgment. Our lives are set on the boundary between the kingdom of God and the kingdom of evil. The old formula stating that the Christian may be *in* the world but not *of* the world is not strictly true. Whether we like it or not, we are all involved in the kingdom of *this* world. We have a dual citizenship. Like some of the ancient Jews who were citizens of Rome, yet subjects of the Lord, we are participants of the "colony of heaven," yet we are set also within the commonwealth of this evil world. When Jesus said: "Render to Caesar the things that are Caesar's, and to God the things that are God's" (Mark 12:17, RSV), He declared the reality of *both* kingdoms. In His temptations He lived at the fused edge where they both met. Luke

---

[20] P. T. Forsyth, *The Justification of God* (London: Independent Press, Ltd., 1917), p. 183.

has this pregnant expression: "When the Devil had exhausted every kind of temptation, he withdrew until his next opportunity." (Luke 4:13)

It is a part of the Christian kerygma that the kingdom as final judgment has not as yet destroyed the kingdom of evil. The two now exist side by side. They may be said to overlap, or even to flow into one another, until neither goodness nor evil is ever found in pure form. The world is so much with us that we never find goodness wholly uncorrupted, nor do we ever find evil quite as unmixed as it might conceivably be. We often speak of goodness tainted with evil. Why not also speak of evil as adulterated with good? The two kingdoms interpenetrate each other much like the meeting of two currents in a river—never totally distinct, yet never completely identical. As Stewart dramatically says: "The two ages had overlapped; time was shot through with eternity; and gleams of glory were continually piercing and scattering the darkness of sinful history." [21]

The traditional doctrine of prevenient grace safeguards two necessary elements in man's relation to God: first, it indicates that man is totally unable, in his own wisdom and strength, to turn to God or exhibit a righteous life. But, on the other hand, it declares that a measure of righteousness has been conferred upon every man as a divine gift whereby he is enabled, if he will, to repent and turn to God. Thus in spite of his natural moral perversity, man has this gracious mark of God's care so indelibly graven upon him that he cannot be thoroughly happy in sin. But there is also the truth of the prevenience of evil. I am not sure I should want to call it prevenient disgrace, but there is a dark shadow over the soul of each of us. We are participants in the "gonewrongness" of others. More truly than we like to admit we all reap the consequences of

---

[21] James S. Stewart, *Thine is the Kingdom* (New York: Charles Scribner's Sons, 1956), p. 30.

the sins of those who have gone before us—unto the fourth and fifth generations, and beyond.

This involvement comes home to each of us. We participate in the benefits of evil. Our lives are advantaged through the injustices others often must endure. Our freedom lacks some of its glamor when we know that thousands of displaced persons exist hardly above the subsistence level. Refugee camps become the breeding places of apprehension lest the free world's cry of democracy be found an empty echo. The education of our children means a little less than it might when we learn that they are taught by money collected from the liquor industry. Our very food is on occasion produced by laborers living in virtual peonage. Our pride in the brotherhood of the Christian ministry is rebuked when Negro ministers receive less than their due, simply because their skins are black. Judgment should begin at the house of the Lord.

At times we may condition ourselves to ignore this flowing together of the kingdom of God and the kingdom of evil. Yet there is an even greater danger, which is to come to terms with the mingling of right with wrong. Stewart quotes a penetrating line from Forsyth: "One reason why the Church is too little missionary is that it is established on good terms with its world instead of being a foreign mission from another." Then he adds: "The powers of darkness will never be scattered by a Christendom infiltrated by the enemy; and a religion that is to redeem the perishing must itself be uncompromising in its allegiance to the Redeemer." [22]

In this current involvement, no dreamy optimism about the future is adequate. We dare not be complacent. The genius of the Gospel is that it produces both the mood of commitment to the will of God and a protest against the kingdom of this world. As Phillips paraphrases St. Paul: "Don't let the

---

[22] *Ibid.,* pp. 19f.

world around you squeeze you into its own mold, but let God remold your minds from within." (Romans 12:2)

This mood of involvement is found within the new scientific concern. The scientist is no mere spectator; his destiny is wrapped up with his researches. Yet the scientist is also a vital part of the world which he observes. It has been well said that the most significant object is at the *small* end of the telescope. History likewise must be seen from the viewpoint of one who participates in it. But it is in religion that this involvement reaches its climax. To speak of God demands that I be committed to my affirmations. The early formulators of the kerygma were not mere announcers, or heralds even of the divine deed. They personally participated in those deeds so that they could say: "God was in Christ personally reconciling the world to Himself—not counting their sins against them—and has commissioned us with the message of reconciliation." Note: God's action in the reconciliation includes also those who have experienced the reconciliation. They are "now Christ's ambassadors, as though God were appealing" to men through them. (II Corinthians 5:19f)

As declared in the kerygma, God is seen as "participating in our human sorrow and tragedy and therefore able to redeem it from within." The Cross is to be seen then "as the act by which God involves himself in the fate of our humanity, at whatever cost to himself." [23]

NO ACADEMIC ANSWERS

This is certain: there is no academic answer adequate to clarify our predicament in this conflict of kingdoms. It may be we shall come to see we are more endangered by scholars who

---

[23] E. L. Allen, "A Theology of Involvement," *Theology Today*, vol. xi, No. 2 (July, 1954), p. 186. (Printed with permission of *Theology Today*.)

think they know so much, than by wicked men whose evil is so obvious.

If we learn anything from so-called Existentialism, it is that the pursuit of purely rational disciplines alone cannot meet life's most pressing problems. This, I take it, is what Professor Tillich means by saying that the source of the theologian's knowledge is not the universal logos but the Logos who "became flesh." [24] With all the value of sociological studies of family relations, the deepest dimension of meaning is still beyond the reach of scientific, philosophical, empirical methods, that is, any sort of academic study. The family bowed in prayer with the Holy Bible in the midst, is still the clearest insight into the meaning of an authentic home.

Throughout the history of Christian thought theology has often succumbed to the temptation to permit the dynamic of the Gospel to become frozen in an intellectualistic system. It occurred within the Hellenistically inspired Alexandrian Fathers. The most glaring defection came in the rigidities of Thomistic Scholasticism, but the same fault can also be found outside Roman theology. Even an evangelical concern for the Gospel, when it capitulates to the letter of orthodoxy, reveals the inadequacy of academic answers. But again throughout history there have been those who have known the Gospel in terms not of ideas but of living events—Augustine, Pascal, Luther, Kierkegaard, Wesley—all the great theologians of grace.

So persuaded is Dean Stanley R. Hopper of the failure of mere academic answers that he overstated this thesis by saying: "There is no place for systematic theology." And he said this in the interest, not of an irresponsible irrationalism, but of clarification of theological meanings.

What is beyond this academic failure? It might be suggested in the current slogan, "commitment," or the more evangelical

---

[24] Paul Tillich, *Systematic Theology,* vol. i (Chicago: The University of Chicago Press, 1951), p. 16. (Copyright 1951 by the University of Chicago.)

term, "surrender." The appeal is made to stand up and be counted—not so much to *find* the answer as to *be* the answer. This means we are driven by the sheer confusion of the time, even if we are not impelled by the authority of the Gospel, to resist the temptation of anaemic toleration. It is reported that a Texan once built three swimming pools: one with hot water, one with cold water, and one with no water—for people unable to swim. What may be tolerated, even enjoyed, in swimming pools, is dangerous in religion. A genial, romantic, latitudinarian gregariousness produces not only theological sterility but moral confusion. We can attempt to become all things to all men until we become nothing to anyone.

The intellectual climate of our time does not encourage great convictions. A life-and-death commitment to the Gospel is not our characteristic mood.

An eccentric British preacher once remarked that the Gospel has degenerated until it means little more than a pious exhortation to take good care of Granny and the cat. The words of John Wesley, "we think and let think," are often used in a manner which belies his meaning. But the most important reference is in his treatise, "The Character of a Methodist." The full statement is: "But as to *all opinions which do not strike at the root of Christianity,* we think and let think." [25] His ecumenical sympathies are well-known, carefully elucidated in such sermons as: "Caution Against Bigotry," and "Catholic Spirit." But he would never agree to dull the cutting edge of deep redemptive convictions and thereby destroy the faith.[26]

What would have happened if the Philippian jailor had confronted this shallow mood of tolerance? To his question, "What must I do to be saved?" (Acts 16:30), imagine these answers:

---

25 John Wesley, *The Works of the Rev. John Wesley,* vol. viii (London, Wesley Conference Office, 1872), p. 340. [Italics mine]

26 See: John Wesley, Sermons: "A Caution Against Bigotry," "Catholic Spirit," in *Wesley's Standard Sermons,* Edward H. Sugden, Editor (London: The Epworth Press, 1931), vol. ii, pp. 104, 126.

"We'll appoint a committee." "Let's conduct a survey." "Suppose we ventilate the problem." "There are, you know, several schools of thought on the subject." Or: "What do *you* think?"

In his Gifford Lectures, W. Macneile Dixon has left to us a most refreshing analysis of "The Human Situation." He speaks of the mind of man, the power of reason, asking if it can possibly adjudicate all controversies, terminate all disputes. He goes on to show that even eminent thinkers "have troubled the waters of thought only to muddy them." [27] Scientific or philosophical objectivity is a phantom so far as the most crucial questions of life are concerned. Reason is not the only fundamental thing about us. "The intellect seems to stand in its own light, reducing all it contemplates to the shadowiness of its self-chosen concepts, and by its own confession we can know nothing more than these, its peculiar creation." [28] The basic fact is that we are alive, conscious persons, living centers not to be circumscribed by mere academic analysis. "The most fundamental thing is that we are living beings, and purposeful beings, and very complicated beings, of whom reason is an attribute, an instrument, but most obviously not the whole of us." [29]

What, then, is the clue to certainty? How to move beyond this thin mood of tolerance—as if nothing ultimately matters— even beyond the position that what ultimately matters is purely rational? Dixon in a manner anticipates the Existentialists. He argues that the most powerful force in making history is the metaphor, the figure of speech, the symbol or sign pointing to the living reality. Thus religious commitment, or, as we have been saying, involvement in a dynamic meeting at the place where the Divine and the Demonic intersect, is a valid clue to

---

[27] W. Macneile Dixon, *The Human Situation* (New York: Macmillan & Co., Ltd., and St. Martin's Press, Inc.), p. 54.

[28] *Ibid.*, p. 64.

[29] *Ibid.*, p. 64.

the meaning of life. To be sure, reason must be utilized as we attempt to communicate the significance of the meeting. As an instrument of the self, here the religious self, it is indispensable. But it cannot account for its own presence; rather, it is accounted for by the self who uses it. To paraphrase Pascal: "The self has its reasons which the reason does not understand."

A SENSE OF WHAT IS VITAL

If then there can be no final resting place in academic answers to our involvement in the conflict of kingdoms, what hope is there for the preacher of kerygmatic theology? Moffatt's vivid paraphrase of Paul's message to the Philippian Church is well known: He prayed that these Christians might have, among other things, "a sense of what is vital." (Philippians 1:9, Moffatt)

The presence of the kingdom, here and now, as final judgment, and our necessary involvement in it, requires that we discriminate between the marginal and the central. As Reinhold Niebuhr once remarked: "Christianity has few absolutes, but the absolutes which are absolute are absolute."

Half a century ago a Lyman Beecher Lecturer designated one of the cardinal sins of the church as triviality, the preoccupation with littleness. Religion is so easily associated with the small, the negligible. He reminded his hearers that churches become hives of little bees with due proportions of drones and stings, instead of fraternities of godly, great, wise and worthy souls.[30]

I am persuaded we shall never recapture a sense of what is vital until we see how deeply God Himself is involved in our predicament. Here we meet the religion of Incarnation. It is truly said that the only religion adequate to meet the future is the religion of Incarnation, when God is seen as inextricably

---

[30] Forsyth, *Positive Preaching and The Modern Mind, op. cit.,* pp. 170, 174.

involved in human struggles. L. Harold DeWolf has pinpointed this issue:

> God be praised that when He saw the estrangement of men from Him, He did not draw apart from us, to thunder down His word upon us from a distance! He subjected Himself to maximum involvement in the world, with all its sin and pride.[31]

Calvary, then, becomes the index to God's involvement in our need. The theme of the strange fascination of the Cross is often heard. It is set to music. It is built into great cathedrals. It is woven into poetry. It is spread on canvas. It is even planted on crude roadside shrines. But it is in that hour when the Cross becomes personal, for us, that we understand its deeper meaning. Two things happen:

(1) Through death to the old self, we are raised to new life in Christ. "I have been crucified with Christ; it is no longer I who live, but Christ who lives in me; and the life I now live in the flesh I live by faith in the Son of God, who loved me and gave himself for me." (Galatians 2:20 RSV) Whenever we encounter evil in any form, and see it in the light of what it does to God and to His creatures, and dedicate ourselves to do something about it, this becomes our Calvary.

(2) This Cross also produces discontented souls. In days like these, I have come to regard it as little less than treason to the kingdom to seek, or offer, peace of mind. The revised version of the hymn of this mood might be: "Relax, My Soul, Calm Every Nerve!" But why should we desire so easily, without pain, what Our Lord in such agony of struggle obtained through the cross?

I wait for some courageous soul to preach on the theme: "The Virtue of Being Maladjusted"! I am increasingly impatient with the trend toward dull normalcy. I have had a friendly

---

[31] L. Harold DeWolf, "A Theology of Maximum Involvement," *The Drew Gateway* (Winter, 1958), vol. xxviii, No. 2, p. 89.

feud with some friends over what seems an overemphasis upon
psychological analyses for missionary personnel. There is something accursed in the attempt to find missionaries to conform
to an anaemic average. Our effort to concentrate upon candi-
dates who are "safe," who may be depended upon to fit into
a "normal" program, to be a kind of ecclesiastical rubber
stamp, putting into practice whatever may be implied in a
"well-adjusted personality," could be a travesty upon the Gospel which, whatever else it does, produces misfits in a Godless
society. I wonder how St. Paul would have fared under the
scrutiny of a Minnesota multiphasic? No doubt Augustine
would have blown a fuse in a counseling situation. Luther
would likely be classified as a mild paranoid. Possibly St.
Francis would seem too neurotic to minister to sophisticated
minds in a university center. And I have serious question that
Jesus of Nazareth could secure the endorsement of some psychiatrists for the missionary program of the Church.

In fact, I have almost come to believe it is only the misfits,
the queer, as the British would say, the awkward souls, rather
than the pale normal average ciphers, who understand a "sense
of what is vital." John A. Mackay approvingly quotes W. H.
Auden:

> Ruffle the perfect manners of the frozen heart,
> And once again compel it to be awkward and alive.[32]

If we get any direction from history, there is a kind of rugged
daring in those who have lived committed here and now to the
kingdom. When the Rich Young Ruler turned his back upon
Jesus, little did he know he was cutting himself off from the
greatest adventure of history. He chose the death of mediocrity.
History validates the choice of Jesus of Nazareth, who "stead-

---

[32] John A. Mackay, *Christianity on the Frontier* (New York: The Macmillan
Company, 1950), p. 30.

fastly set His face to go to Jerusalem" (Luke 9:51, KJV), as having "a sense of what is vital."

GOD AS AVAILABLE

It was the invasion of the historical process of this world by the kingdom of God which produced the crisis through which Christians have lived. Our Lord interpreted this conflict of kingdoms as the downfall of evil: "I was watching and saw Satan fall from heaven like a flash of lightning!" (Luke 10:18) Jesus understood Himself as the Deliverer who entered the Strong Man's house "and conquers him." (Luke 11:21f) He speaks of Himself as by the finger of God casting out evil spirits. (Luke 11:20) And in it all He was exercising authority over the demonic powers of the kingdom of evil and at the same time claiming that His Kingdom was not "founded in this world." (John 18:36)

This action of Christ was a testimony that God was with man and ever available. The purpose of Christ's advent was not so much to tell men about the kingdom of God as to demonstrate it in action. His behaviour "shows us the kingdom of God at war with the kingdom of evil, with Jesus spearheading the attack." [33] Or, as Preiss puts it: "At the very moment when the Son of Man accepts death, there takes place in the presence of God the decisive event: Satan is cast out. He whose name means 'accuser' is banished from the divine presence. That is the judgment of this world. The dominion of Satan is shattered." [34]

No one has more clearly interpreted this available action of God in the victory of Christ over Satan than has Professor Kümmel. Jesus' vision of the "fall" of Satan rightly belongs "to the oldest tradition" in the Gospel structure. And its mean-

---

[33] Hunter, *Introducing New Testament Theology, op. cit.,* p. 18.
[34] Preiss, *op. cit.,* pp. 18f.

ing is well understood within the Jewish framework of the conquest of evil by God through the action of the Messiah. This conquest has already occurred. Satan has been deprived of his power. His rule is broken. This could have meant only one thing to Jesus: "The defeat accomplished in the fight he is waging victoriously against the devils." Thus Kümmel concludes:

> So here too it is quite firmly established that the eschatological consummation, the Kingdom of God, has already become a present reality in the ministry of Jesus. And here too the message of the approaching Kingdom of God is actually illuminated by the knowledge that through Jesus' activities the future consummation is brought into the present.[35]

C. S. Lewis has said that there are only two kinds of people in the world: those who say to God: "Thy will be done," and those to whom God says *"Thy* will be done." [36] It is the confidence of the Christian man that the moral structure of the universe will not let him down—since it is rooted in the dependability of a righteous, personal God. Simon Peter understood the alternatives, though at times he did not live by them. "It is our duty to obey the orders of God rather than the orders of men." (Acts 5:29) Thus the claim: "We cannot help speaking about what we have actually seen and heard!" (Acts 4:20) This was a new dimension of motivation. It came direct from heaven to man's soul. This was the priority of God over all Caesars. God was available. Hence He would be obeyed.

Into this perishing order of this world there has been introduced, in the total meaning of the Advent of Christ, the imperishable order of the kingdom of God. There could be

---

35 Kümmel, *Promise and Fulfilment, op. cit.,* p. 114.
36 C. S. Lewis, *The Great Divorce* (New York: The Macmillan Company, 1955), p. 69.

no compromise, no coming to terms with evil. As Bishop New-bigin vividly describes it:

> The new age and the present age, the reign of God and the reign of the prince of this world, cannot openly confront each other without one destroying the other. By his taking of human nature upon Himself and living a human life in this world, Christ has exposed Himself to all the powers of this dark world and they have combined to destroy Him. But by this deed He has taken upon Himself the whole curse of sin, manifested the righteousness of God, and broken the grip of Satan upon us.[37]

The theme of the Evanston Assembly of the World Council of Churches was "The Christian Hope." But the thing which keeps hope alive is the experienced availability of God, ever present within the struggles of every evil situation. In *The Screwtape Letters,* written supposedly by an older and wiser devil to his earth-bound nephew, C. S. Lewis has Screwtape express the fear which lurks in hell that human beings may remain loyal to God—in spite of pain, defeat, and the silences of heaven. And the cause of evil, of hell, is never more in jeopardy than when a human "looks round upon a universe from which every trace of Him seems to have vanished, and asks why he has been forsaken, *and still obeys.*" [38]

In the theology of the kerygma, whatever else was pro-claimed, the primitive Christians were certain that the king-dom of God had, in Jesus Christ, come down out of heaven for men. They now were living in the eschaton. They were enlisted in the Battle of Armageddon. The last judgment had begun. The crises of history could not be solved by academic discipline but by an overwhelming "sense of what is vital."

---

[37] Lesslie Newbigin, *The Household of God* (New York: Friendship Press, 1954), p. 126.

[38] C. S. Lewis, *The Screwtape Letters* (London: Geoffrey Bles, 1946), p. 47. [Italics mine]

And throughout it all was the daily experience of an ever-available God. As Jesus said: "You will find trouble in the world—but, never lose heart, I have conquered the world!" (John 16:33)

THREE

The Sacrament Of Death

Even for the biologist, death is a mystery. Why an organism should disintegrate and return to the earth is a recognized but unexplained fact. The philosopher may always be "pursuing death and dying" and he has "reason to be of good cheer when he is about to die." But, admittedly, according to Socrates, he has "not found out either what is the nature of that death which the true philosopher deserves." [1]

> Come lovely and soothing death,
> Undulate round the world, serenely arriving, arriving,
> In the day, in the night, to all, to each,
> Sooner or later delicate death.[2]

---

[1] Plato, *The Dialogues of Plato*, vol. i, *Phaedo*, 64, B. Jowett, Translator (New York: Oxford University Press, Inc., Random House edition, 1937), p. 447.
[2] Walt Whitman, *Leaves of Grass* (New York: David McKay Co., Inc.), p. 260.

But there is serious doubt that Whitman actually regarded death as quite that "delicate." If he did, he stands almost solitary among men.

The burial service asks a question which it never answers: "Lord, let me know mine end, and the number of my days; that I may be certified how long I have to live." (Psalm 39:1, *The Book of Common Prayer*) Indeed, that same service reminds us of the frailty of life: "Man, that is born of woman, hath but a short time to live, and is full of misery. He cometh up, and is cut down, like a flower; he fleeth as it were a shadow, and never continueth in one stay."

I am persuaded no philosophy, no religion, is adequate unless it has some sure word about death. It may not be the final word; only death itself has that—or One who has conquered death—but to hear nothing but silence when the heart is strained to catch even a whisper, this is as frustrating as death itself. How, then, does "The Sacrament of Death" fit into the theology of the kerygma?

In Dodd's thesis the "age of fulfillment" "has taken place through the ministry, death, and resurrection of Jesus." [3] Since Dodd considers the resurrection as a separate element in the kerygma, it seems wise here to focus attention upon the death of Our Lord. However, His death is best seen as set within the context of death as a human phenomenon. Thus, before considering the sacramental character of the Cross, some preliminary items need to be seen.

REFLECTIONS ON DYING

Suppose we survey some of the certainties of death, even before attempting to seek its meaning. For one thing, the most

---

[3] Dodd, *The Apostolic Preaching and Its Developments*, *op. cit.*, p. 38f.

certain fact of life is death. This is the one absolute human inevitability.

Of course, we find it hard to accept the fact of death with equanimity. It always pushes into our lives like an alien intruder. But no door is devised to keep it out. We occasionally speak of private pain. In an even more profound sense we may speak of private death. There is no other kind. There may be a fellowship of suffering, but no fellowship of dying. "You must walk the lonesome valley; you must go there by yourself." And yet, no living person has ever experienced death. A person may be legally dead and still live, may even be medically dead and yet live. But this merely means that he is *not* dead.

Also, death is a necessary fact of life. The death of the individual is needed to perpetuate the race. To think of a world where death never came would be horrifying—sooner or later we should be pushing each other off whatever uninhabited bits of land were left. The present population explosion raises serious questions about the future food supply —what would it be if every bird, beast, fish, and man ever born were still alive! As a friend of mine once said, it is much better that the many shall live for awhile and then make room for others than for a few to live all the time.

The Dean of American Philosophers, W. E. Hocking, remarks that death is necessary lest each new generation be completely submerged by the "wisdom" (?) and authority of maturity. Death makes it unnecessary forever to educate the old in new ways, "for as the old men pass, the rigid formulae pass with them." He continues:

> If there were no natural death, society might well be driven to institute some form of artificial death, such as an honorable ostracism, lest the cumulative weight of great authority hold all new-arriving tongues locked in deference and thwart their arrival at maturity through the exercise of responsible opinion....

It is not merely that the old become static—that need not be the case—but they frequently become wise and prudent. And life must progress in part by the imprudence of those who undertake the impossible, not knowing what they do.[4]

Furthermore, there is a tragic element in death. Death seems to be a contradiction of all that we cherish as having value in life, and we find it hard to believe that this frustration can be intended. We know we must die that others may live, whether others live or not; yet it always comes as an unwanted visitor, sounding a tragic note.

In fact, all our efforts to prolong life, to make it better, are eventually doomed to fail. It is no accident that death is often portrayed as laughing at us. I am part of a university with one of the finest medical schools in America. But I never enter the buildings without the thought: every ministry here, in the end, is destined to one thing—failure. The best each and all of the most skilled scientists of the world can do is to make life a little more comfortable and last a little longer. The death rate continues to stand at 100%. Do not misunderstand me; I am grateful for this and regularly seek such aid. I am in no hurry to investigate the next life. But I know, as does every medical man, that death will have its final word.

Again, man is the only creature that knows he must die, and also the only creature which doubts its finality. I like the way John Whale says it when he refers to *dying* as a biological fact but *having to die* as a human fact.[5] Thus, death can never be regarded simply as a natural event. It is because we doubt the finality of death that we resist it. Somehow we feel we are never prepared for death; it interrupts us, either in our own lives or in those of our loved ones. In some mysterious manner we regard death as an enemy. Indeed, Paul has called it the

---

4 William Ernest Hocking, *Thoughts on Death and Life* (New York: Harper & Brothers, 1938), p. 14.
5 Whale, *Christian Doctrine, op. cit.,* p. 174.

"last enemy." It would not be so cruel were death only the end of the things which we dislike. But it brings home to us the impermanence both of the things we despise and the things we love.

And yet, it is impossible to think of ourselves as dead. For thinking about it means I am a spectator, a witness. Yet death by definition means we cannot be present to observe it, or else we have survived it. But we have no eyewitness report from beyond death. This is another evidence of the incomprehensible nature of our world; about those places of which we ask the most insistent questions, we find no answer. But this also implies that there is a permanent quality in personality which even death cannot touch.

Finally, it is possible for life to lose its meaning—for ourselves. We can come to the place where we just do not care. That is, we just do not care about *our* life, and death. Bertrand Russell, in *What I Believe,* put it rather bluntly: "I believe that when I die I shall rot, and nothing of my ego will survive. I am not young, and I love life. But I should scorn to shiver with terror at the thought of annihilation." [6] And even Luther, near the end of his life, could write: "I will no longer tarry, but set myself to go to Wittenberg and there lay myself in a coffin and give the worms a fat doctor to feed upon." [7] But while we can take such an attitude toward ourselves, we cannot be so casual about the death of our loved ones. We may even feel the judgment of our personal wickedness and know that we deserve to die; but we cannot desire the total destruction of those we love. As John Baillie has said so well:

Perhaps in certain moods I can contemplate my own death and say, 'I do not care whether that is the end of me or not; the thing

---

[6] Bertrand Russell, *What I Believe* (New York: E. P. Dutton & Co., Inc., 1925), p. 13.

[7] Quoted from Julius Köstlin, *Life of Luther,* translated from the German (New York: Charles Scribner's Sons, 1883), p. 576.

does not interest me.' But surely in *no* mood can I contemplate the death of the most precious soul I know, the death of him whom I most love and reverence, and say, 'I do not care whether that is the end of *him* or not; the thing does not interest me' . . .

No man who was not a cad could stand by his beloved's deathbed and say (or think) that he was not interested in immortality. Try only to picture him, saying not merely, 'For all I know' (which an honest man might well be forced to say) but, 'For all I know *or care,* this is the end of you, my dear!' [8]

THE DEMOCRACY OF DEATH

Philip of Macedon is reported to have instructed a slave to come into his presence daily and say: "Philip, remember that thou must die." Slave or master, jester or monarch—death reminds each that there is no indispensable man. The drama of this democracy is seen in the Moravian cemetery, where all stones are alike—flat ones each the same shape and size. We are so conditioned by all sorts of experienced inequalities that we easily ignore this leveling process of death.

But it is this very democracy of death which raises certain questions. Ideally we should like to believe that there is a sort of common character among all men. Yet the very fact that death reaps with such utter disregard for the distinctions which we make, reminds us that death often operates upon those who never had a chance to live. When we think of the multitudes now alive who will never know satisfied hunger, when we recall that other millions are exploited by various types of discrimination, when we know that many of our comforts are to some extent possible because of the inconveniences and even suffering of others—the very democracy of death becomes to us our judgment. It affords little solace to know that the lofty as well as the low require the same space when dead,

---

[8] John Baillie, *And the Life Everlasting* (New York: Charles Scribner's Sons, 1951), pp. 62f.

if our greed or indifference contributes to those things which destroy hope among those who, while alive physically, never know what the abundant life really means.

But again, it is this very element of injustice which argues that death does not have the final word.

DEATH AND JUDGMENT

May it be that judgment has lost much of its meaning because we have relegated it to that mysterious period after death? I have come to feel we should think of final judgment not as some future crisis but as the ultimate measure of all human life by the Passion of Our Lord. For judgment, after all, is quite as pertinent to the way we live now as to some period after we die. Thus we say the final judgment has already appeared in history; there is nothing more final than the "Lamb on the throne." It has been said no better than by the late P. T. Forsyth:

> The Cross of Christ is God's last judgment on all sin, for its destruction by a realm of infinite grace and love. It is the last resource of the Almighty Holiness; and *His* last resource is the end of all things— which is now always at hand in a kingdom both coming and come. . . . The 'last judgment' is but a time expression of this ultimate judgment, now inherent, perpetual, and fundamental. Ever since, human history has been living in this final judgment, and living it out.[9]

The new feature in Christianity was this—that the final judgment was closely associated, and even identified, with the work of the historic Christ.

How does death confront us with judgment? For one thing, it dramatizes the shortness of time. The longer we live the faster time seems to move. The contrast between two New

---

[9] Forsyth, *The Justification of God, op. cit.,* pp. 183, 190.

Testament words for time suggests the brevity of it: one word is *chronos,* which refers to measured duration, successiveness, clock or calendar time. The other is *kairos,* which suggests opportunity, a suitable season, an appropriate moment for action. "Behold, now is the acceptable time; behold, now is the day of Salvation." (II Corinthians 6:2, RSV) The precious present is not to be lavishly squandered; each hour has in it an element of destiny.

> While man is growing, life is in decrease;
> And cradles rock us nearer the tomb.
> Our birth is nothing but our death begun.[10]

Death is also a judgment upon the frailty of life. The Bible speaks of life as a "vapor," a "cloud," a "step" between life and death. The silver cord is so easily snapped and the pitcher quickly breaks at the fountain—and the dust returns to earth once more. "In the midst of life we are in death" is the constant reminder that life is a delicate thread so easily broken.

Death furthermore exposes in judgment the cruelty of the world. Somehow the romanticist fails to grapple with the harsher realities of life. What may be in nature mere indifference to human welfare carries with it a ruin which suggests even a demonic power. We appreciate the Christian insight of Maltbie D. Babcock in inspiring us to sing, "This is My Father's World." But we cannot forget that the author himself fell into such deep despair that he took his own life.

But especially is death judgment upon our own self-sufficiency. Nothing more effectively destroys our prideful confidence in our own ability than the threat of extinction.

---

10 Edward Young, *Night Thoughts on Life, Death, and Immortality,* 3rd revised edition (New York: A. S. Barnes & Co., 1854), Night v. Line 717.

Oh why should the spirit of mortal be proud?
Like a fast-flitting meteor, a fast-flying cloud,
A flash of the lightning, a break of the wave,
He passes from life to his rest in the grave.[11]

SIN AND DEATH

The usual interpretation of sin and death is that the latter is due to the former. At least, the traditional view both of Genesis and Paul is that death is the consequence of sin. As for Genesis, it is doubtful if the story warrants our inference that men were created immortal. In fact, when God said to Adam and Eve: "Dust thou art, and unto dust thou shalt return," He implied that they were created subject to death. This is not a pronouncement of penalty but a statement of fact. Their sin lay in their refusal to accept their human mortality, and their desire to be like God. Thus we see why they were driven from the Garden: "Behold, the man has become like one of us, knowing good and evil; and now, *lest he put forth his hand and take also of the tree of life, and eat, and live forever*—therefore the Lord God sent him forth from the Garden of Eden, to till the ground from which he was taken." (Genesis 3:22f., RSV)

Notice two things: (1) What man "gained" in the "fall" is more significant than what he "lost"; that is, he gained the knowledge of the distinction between good and evil. This is one evidence of man's Godlikeness—"like one of us, knowing good and evil." Only a creature who knows this distinction can become truly saintly, for saintliness means deliverance from sinfulness—but only a person who knows himself sinful can be so delivered. (2) But also this creature of God threatened to "take of the tree of life, and eat, and live forever" —meaning that he did not then possess immortality.

---

[11] William Knox, "Mortality," from "Songs of Israel."

As for Romans 5:12f, in the absence of other specific indications of the causal relation between sin and death, scholars feel that Paul was simply reflecting the Rabbinical teaching of his time. But is there some further explanation of the relation between sin and death? Is it possible that death may well be regarded as part, even a necessary part, of the world which God created and called good? Death would then be the normal transition from this life, as a sort of period of preparation, into the fuller future life with God. Sin's entrance distorted this "natural" movement from this life into the next by making man unfit for fellowship with God. Thus the very normal function of death, as we have set forth previously, would itself be distorted. As Professor G. B. Caird has said: "Evil has perverted even death." [12] Thus we can allow evil to be a power which has so twisted the normal function of death, for example, to permit one generation to leave the stage of life honorably, and to make room for another, until death, instead of being a friend, is referred to as an "enemy." It is, indeed, the "last enemy" since it has perverted the function of the divinely ordered means of transition from this life into the next.

We must not overlook, however, the sense in which sin actually *is* the cause of death. Biblically, sin is used in a metaphorical sense to refer to spiritual death. Sin by its very nature breeds suspicion, bitterness, mistrust, selfishness, and these preclude any true spiritual life since they leave no room for God. There is an inescapable truth in the existential argument here. Thus Tillich regards man as naturally mortal, and "man comes from dust and returns to dust." Only as he partakes of the "tree of life" does he possess eternal life. "Participation in the eternal makes man eternal; separation from the eternal leaves man in his natural finitude." [13] Hence, the "estrange-

---

12 G. B. Caird, *The Truth of the Gospel*, A Primer of Christianity, part iii (New York: Oxford University Press, 1950), p. 82.

13 Paul Tillich, *Systematic Theology*, vol. ii (Chicago: The University of Chicago Press, 1957), p. 67. (Copyright 1957 by University of Chicago.)

ment" of man from God carries the sting of death since "it transforms the anxious awareness of one's having to die into the painful realization of a lost eternity. . . . Under the condition of estrangement, anxiety about death is more than anxiety about annihilation. It makes death an evil, a structure of destruction." [14] Or, as Bultmann puts it:

> Man, called to selfhood, tries to live out of his own strength and thus loses his self—his 'life'—and rushes into death. This is the domination of sin: All man's doing is directed against his true intention—viz. to achieve life. . . .
>
> He who derives life out of the transitory must, himself, perish with the perishing of the transitory.[15]

But the thing which makes the relation of sin and death most disturbing is not that death is inevitable; but that, in our own self-reliant attempt to find life apart from the only source of life, God, we know that we deserve to die. "You are not willing to come to Me to have real life!" (John 5:40) The profound treatment in the Fourth Gospel of the idea of the source of life being in God carries the corollary that those who do not receive this conferred life from Him, abide in death. It is not that in our most depraved condition we know we deserve to die because we are wicked; it is, rather, because in our polite and self-willed indifference we feel no need of God, we forfeit the only right to live.

THE SACRAMENT OF DEATH

The idea of the sufferings of God has been proposed. May we now take a step further and speak of God as experiencing the fact of death? I hear horrified opposition crying "Crude

---

[14] *Ibid.*, p. 68.
[15] Bultmann, *Theology of the New Testament*, vol. i, *op. cit.*, pp. 246f.

anthropomorphism." But before we reject it, let us look at the idea. Suppose we consider the experience of death as the divine sacrament in which this last enemy of man is not only known and experienced, but actually *used* as a vehicle to destroy it.

The sacramental principle is that the material is used as a vehicle to convey the spiritual. The lesser is used by the greater to carry a significance the lesser alone could never portray. This seems to be the widespread motif not only in Christianity but in all religions; the physical is instrumental to the spiritual. This is necessary, possibly, because we live in a world in which our lives constitute the convergence of the material and the spiritual. Man is of the earth, earthy; he also is made in the "Image of God." But since man is not pure spirit (whatever that would be), he must as a being who is not pure spirit constantly use the material as an instrument of the spiritual. Indeed, man's own body is a particular example of this fact.

This principle is not limited to religion. It is seen in the arts where canvas and paint yield to the perspective of the soul of the artist to convey truth by means of inanimate things. In music it is the combination of sounds, silences, and variations. It is seen in science where truth is expressed in symbols. History itself may be regarded as sacramental; in that through events the meaning of human life is dramatized and recorded. Culture may be seen as the storehouse of the past transmitted to the present in a manner which may be called sacramental. Even creation may be understood as the action of God to express His mind, an effort in which "His invisible nature, namely, His eternal power and deity, has been clearly perceived in the things that have been made." (Romans 1:20, RSV) The same idea has been expressed philosophically by A. A. Bowman in *A Sacramental Universe.*[16]

---

16 A. A. Bowman, *A Sacramental Universe* (Princeton: Princeton University Press, 1939).

The supreme example of this sacramental principle is that of the Incarnation of God in Christ. It is set forth most beautifully in the Prologue to the Fourth Gospel:

> In the beginning was the Word, and the Word was with God; and the Word was God. He was in the beginning with God; all things were made through him, and without him was not anything made that was made. In him was life, and the life was the light of men. The light shines in the darkness, and the darkness has not overcome it. . . . And the Word became flesh and dwelt among us, full of grace and truth; we have beheld his glory, glory as of the only Son from the Father. (John 1:1-4, 14, RSV)

But it is not sufficient to see God's sacramental activity limited to Christ's Incarnation. Creation and redemption must ever be kept close together, since they are two sides of the same divine purpose. If the Incarnation be understood as God stepping into the ranks of that humanity which is destined to die, the Death of Christ may be understood as the drama of deliverance from that death. If He came in the "form of a servant" "for us men and our salvation," His death is the logic of His coming—as Irenaeus, Luther, and Emil Brunner would say, the Incarnation was completed upon the Cross.[17]

It is beyond the limits of our present subject to give a complete philosophy of Calvary. Only an outline can be suggested. But this must be regarded as fundamental: In some profound sense it would seem needful for God to enter fully into the soiled, frustrated, death-ridden existence of men. It is one thing for Him to contemplate the misery of men from the comparative security of heaven. It is another thing that

> He, who had always been God by nature, did not cling to His prerogatives as God's equal, but stripped Himself of all privilege

---

[17] Emil Brunner, *The Christian Doctrine of Creation and Redemption*, Dogmatics, vol. ii, Translated by Olive Wyon (Philadelphia: The Westminster Press, 1952), p. 363.

by consenting to be a slave by nature and being born as mortal man. And, having become man, He humbled Himself by living a life of utter obedience, even to the extent of dying, *and the death he died was the death of a common criminal.* (Philippians 2:5ff)

That this is, in our day, as it was in Paul's—both a stone of stumbling to Jews, a scandal to Greeks, and absurdity to the worldly-wise, is quite evident. But that it is the certainty of the Gospel we must not deny. Upon seeing a picture of Jesus upon the Cross and hearing the story, a lad said: "I bet if God had been there, He wouldn't have let it happen." But that's just the point: God *was* there. He was there in a more profound sense than anyone else.

The Lenten subject annually brings to us its own temptations: first, to see the Cross as only the calculating cruelty of wicked or ignorant men. There was religious fanaticism there. Had Jesus not disregarded the Law? Had He not broken the Sabbath? Had He not jeopardized the Temple? Had He not consorted with publicans and sinners? Had He not claimed a divineness possessed only by Yahweh? Of course, wicked men were there. And so was political conspiracy, both Jewish and Roman. He had spoken of a kingdom. Neither the throne of David nor that of the Caesars could tolerate a rival. And the mob was there, a mob maintained, probably in this case, by the minority. The voice was the voice of the crowd; but the hands were the hands of Caiaphas and his henchmen.

Yes, the death of Christ is often viewed as due solely to the scheming of wicked men, the crucifixion as the convergence of Jewish bigotry and Roman cruelty. Certainly it is true that a man with convictions contrary to his time is always in danger. Yet this is not the Calvary of Our Lord. If the Cross was only the accidental or fateful encounter of a devoted religious enthusiast, so dedicated to His ideals as to suffer for them, it matters little what we say during Passion Week.

Some may object to this, but it must be confidently affirmed: the Cross was God's way of facing the moral ruin of the world by personally participating in it. God would thrust Himself into the vortex of evil in order to take into His own experience the struggle between right and wrong. This may be dismissed from mind as the poetic fancy of Dante or Milton, yet to do this is to surrender any hope of understanding Calvary. In the Person of Jesus Christ, the Divine Life felt the full impact of all that is meant by sin, death, and the Devil. This is the divine experience of that awful aloneness into which sin ultimately consigns the lost soul. Possibly the climax of this "experience" of God was the Cry of Dereliction: "My God, My God, why hast thou forsaken me?" (Matthew 27:46, RSV) Here was the Divine anguish arising from personal struggle with the powers of evil, undergoing the utter diremption, the tearing apart, the Holy hurt of cosmic travail, bearing the wound which such an encounter always leaves. And the depth of the wound is always measured by the holiness of the life attacked. Hence, in Christ, when perfect holiness and the full fury of Hell met in mortal encounter—there was a dimension of pain never known before within the bounds of human history.

At that place in the universe where the strategy of evil had been most evident, in the life of man, here was the chosen battlefield for God's attack. Dare we say—this was the necessary place for the victory of God if He would keep the respect of the men who are His own creation? For a God who stops short of this complete identification with our predicament is a God with no message for us at the place of our greatest need. This means that the God of the Christian Faith is the God who "cares." And this caring is indelibly stamped upon the total creation—from the smallest seed which is destroyed to produce a harvest, to the holiest love which would suffer to reproduce itself. This means if God would have a creation where values emerge only through suffering, He likewise wills that He par-

ticipate in that suffering. Does this mean that the vivid metaphor in the Apocalypse, "the Lamb slain from the foundation of the world" (Revelation 13:8), affirms that divine pain
as sacrificial love is the very cornerstone of God's creative/
redemptive purpose?

Therefore, the God of the Christian faith is not to be defined first and foremost as the Divinity of the philosophical
systems. He is the God with a broken heart. I like the way
Bishop Stephen Neill refers to one contemplating the horrors
of recent years and then, possibly, saying to God: "Here, at
least you don't understand anything about that." But the
Bishop reminds us that God is entitled to say: "Excuse me, but
having been through it, that is precisely what I do understand." Then the Bishop adds:

> If that is true, I will maintain against all comers that my God,
> deserted, bruised, bleeding, dying, is greater than any other that has
> ever been thought of or imagined or worshipped by man; that this
> God is, in fact, that than which nothing greater can be conceived.[18]

But the significance of death as a sacrament lies in the manner in which it becomes the carrier of God's eternal truth.
This conveys the truth of the Resurrection. We recall our
reference to death being the gateway into eternal life, and to
sin having made us unfit to pass through the gate. We must
resist any attempt to think of the conquest of death by Christ
as mere symbol; rather, we must see it as "something accomplished, something done." And the significance of what He
did is dramatically set forth in the Apocalypse: "Fear not, I
am the first and the last, and the living one; I died, and behold
I am alive for evermore, and I have the keys of Death and
Hades." (Revelation 1:17f RSV)

---

[18] Stephen Neill, *Christian Faith Today* (Baltimore: Penguin Books, 1955), p.
262.

> Thine are these orbs of light and shade;
> Thou madest Life in man and brute;
> Thou madest Death; and lo! Thy foot
> Is on the skull which thou hast made.[19]

This is the divine demonstration that death is not the final word. Man had been deceived into thinking that death was the end, but Jesus went through death and out on the other side into a life forever beyond the reach of death. "We can be sure that the risen Christ never dies again—death's power to touch Him is finished." (Romans 6:9) And it is His promise that "Because I am really alive and you will be alive too." (John 14:19)

The sacrament of death conveys what it signifies:

> That power is the same divine energy which was demonstrated in Christ when He raised Him from the dead and gave Him the place of supreme honour in heaven.... But even though we were dead in our sins God, who is rich in mercy, because of the great love he had for us, gave us life together with Christ.
>
> *Ephesians 1:19; 2:5*

Therefore, we are led to affirm that death itself becomes God's final appeal to men. For in death we are driven to the far edge of despair. All *our* hopes are dashed. This is the final abyss of human frustration. Into it we are thrust with no chance of a late reprieve. Thus may we believe that the faithful Spirit of God, Whose voice every son of man has heard somewhere, in some manner, confronts the doomed soul with one final offer of aid. Might it even be said that this ultimate experience of our creatureliness and helpless sinfulness, becomes God's sacramental agent to turn the impenitent to Himself. It is entirely conceivable that in this manner, if not before, God will ultimately "get" the vast majority of the human race. This is the true sacrament of death!

---

[19] Tennyson, "In Memoriam," Stanza 2.

FOUR

A Door Between Two Worlds

Dorothy Sayers, British author, produced a series of plays on the life of Jesus, for presentation over the British radio. The final play carries the title, "The King Comes to His Own." In her introductory notes, Miss Sayers says: "This play contains a good deal about doors, and knocking at doors. It is, in fact, a play about the door between two worlds." [1] In the Collect for Easter Even, the congregation prays "that through the grave, the gate of death, we may pass to our joyful resurrection."

It is interesting that this "door between two worlds" is a tomb. A tomb once closed, fastened, sealed, and guarded, had been found empty! What had been regarded as a dead

---

[1] Dorothy Sayers, *The Man Born to be King* (London: Victor Gollancz, Ltd., 1946), p. 317.

end had become a corridor with an exit—in life beyond the reach of death. It is the paradox of the Christian faith that the tomb, the place of death, has become the door out into the fuller life. The symbol of the end is now the sign of the beginning. It is no wonder that Luke records: "The Apostles continued to give their witness to the Resurrection of the Lord Jesus with great force, and a wonderful spirit of generosity pervaded the whole fellowship." (Acts 4:33) And Paul implies the answer to his own question: "Why does it seem incredible to you all that God should raise the dead?" (Acts 26:8)

Along with the confession, "Jesus is Lord" (see Romans 10:9 and I Corinthians 12:3), it is now generally recognized that another chief article in the first Christian creed was: the Resurrection of Christ. Barclay may be cited as typical in this judgment:

> It is true to say that the Church itself, and the faith of each individual Christian within it, is founded on belief in the Risen Christ. This is not a late development which was added to the Church's faith, it is there from the very beginning. It was in fact the foundation stone of the Church's faith.[2]

According to Dodd the third element in the kerygma is the resurrection: "By virtue of the resurrection, Jesus has been exalted at the right hand of God, as Messianic head of the new Israel." [3]

Though interpretations may vary as to details, there is practically unanimous agreement that the resurrection was central in the kerygma. Filson regards the resurrection as "the climax of the apostolic preaching." [4] Robinson holds that "historic-

---

[2] William Barclay, *The Mind of St. Paul* (New York: Harper & Brothers; London: William Collins Sons & Co., Ltd., 1958), pp. 113f.

[3] Dodd, *The Apostolic Preaching and Its Developments, op. cit.*, p. 41.

[4] Filson, *Jesus Christ the Risen Lord, op. cit.*, p. 49.

ally speaking, the central content of primitive Christian preaching" was God's eschatological action in the death and resurrection.[5] Howard C. Kee says "the resurrection of Jesus Christ is the presupposition of the apostolic preaching." [6] Barclay refers to the resurrection as "an essential element in that first universal tradition" of the church.[7] Duncan says "the whole of our New Testament Scriptures" is a testimony to the resurrection.[8] Richardson finds in the earliest apostolic tradition a clear witness to the appearances of Jesus after the resurrection, since the resurrection was integral to the church's kerygma.[9] And, again, Bultmann, with all his divergencies from Dodd, speaks of the resurrection as an "article of faith" of the primitive Christians because they found it to be an "eschatological event." And this event originated in the "event of Easter Day." [10]

GOD'S CONQUEST OF EVIL

The resurrection is to be seen as God's conquest of evil. The passage most generally recognized as expressing this victory is Colossians 2:15. The paraphrase by Phillips is, in the writer's judgment, the most vivid underscoring of the divine conquest of evil in the Bible:

> Christ has utterly wiped out the damning evidence of broken laws
> and commandments which always hung over our heads, and has com-

---

[5] Robinson, *A New Quest of the Historical Jesus, op. cit.*, p. 42.

[6] Howard C. Kee, "The Nature and Necessity of the Resurrection According to the New Testament," *The Drew Gateway* (Spring, 1959), Volume xxix, Number 3, p. 169.

[7] Barclay, *op. cit.*, p. 112.

[8] Duncan, *op. cit.*, p. 241.

[9] Alan Richardson, *An Introduction to the Theology of the New Testament* (New York: Harper & Brothers, 1958), p. 192.

[10] Bultmann, *Kerygma and Myth, op. cit.*, pp. 40-42.

pletely annulled it by nailing it over His own Head on the Cross. And then, having drawn the sting of all the powers ranged against us, He exposed them, shattered, empty and defeated, in His final glorious triumphant act!

Colossians 2:14f

It would seem that we have now passed the time for regarding as adequate the view of the Cross as only the exhibition of the love of God. For example, Dodd himself finds that the nearer we reach back into the meaning of the Passion Events themselves, in the peeling away the strata of New Testament interpretation, the more inadequate is the purely "moral" view of Calvary seen to be.[11] And Hodgson, in indicating the abiding value of the doctrine which emphasizes the Cross as a revelation of the love of God, shows himself fully aware that this view, by itself, cannot do justice to the Cross as a manifestation of God's power over sin which has gotten "out of hand." [12] Stewart gives full recognition to the fact that the interpretation of the Cross as moral power does awaken in us a response. But it does more. In the atonement made by Christ something happened "on the divine side, no less than on the human." The deed may have been executed by wicked men, but in an even more profound sense it had been the will of God. Thus Stewart can say: "The cross had been, not God's defeat, but God's purpose and God's victory." [13] Archibald Hunter says the Cross is revelation, and more. It is the self-sacrifice of God in His own involvement in the sins of human life.[14] And Taylor carefully shows the deficiencies of a

---

[11] C. H. Dodd, *According to the Scriptures* (New York: Charles Scribner's Sons; London: James Nisbet and Co., Ltd., 1953), p. 124n.

[12] Leonard Hodgson, *The Doctrine of the Atonement* (New York: Charles Scribner's Sons, 1951), pp. 81, 83.

[13] James S. Stewart, *A Man in Christ* (New York: Harper & Brothers, nd.), pp. 221, 229.

[14] Hunter, *The Work and Words of Jesus, op. cit.,* pp. 99f. See also: *The Message of the New Testament*, p. 115.

moral view of the Cross [15] and then, nearly twenty years later, says:

> We need an objective deed which in its sublimity stands apart from us, something which is there whether we accept it or not, something which is true whether we believe or whether we reject it, a stark irremovable reality which exists in its own right and which owes nothing to ourselves by way of creation or action.[16]

It has remained to a literary figure, to one who is the writer of Christian parables, rather than a professed theologian, to dramatize the moral impact of Calvary upon men. In *That Hideous Strength* C. S. Lewis draws the character of Mark Studdock, a sophisticated professor, ambitious and secular, intent upon academic success and prestige, as he is initiated into a secret British society committed to the task of taking over the institutions and political life of the country. He is participating in the brain-washing necessary to become a member of this inner scientific charmed circle, known as the National Institute of Coordinated Experiments! (N.I.C.E.) The association claims that it reaches back into the mythical past of the land, and possesses the strange powers of Merlin and the Druids. But one thing is imperative: every vestige of past religion and idealism must be erased from the mind, even from the subconscious mind. Thus Mark is taken to the "Objective Room," strangely out of proportion in its claim to scientific objectivity. Upon the floor is a Crucifix! He is instructed to trample upon it, to insult it in various indecent ways. Nevertheless dim memories of a Man who faced the "Crooked" in His day still teased Mark's mind. For Mark recalled that in His day that Man had stood at the place where the Straight met

---

[15] Vincent Taylor, *Jesus and His Sacrifice* (London: Macmillan and Co., Limited; New York: St. Martin's Press, Inc., 1948), pp. 299f.

[16] Vincent Taylor, *The Cross of Christ* (New York: St. Martin's Press, 1956), p. 89.

the Crooked, the normal met the abnormal, the healthy met the diseased. Suddenly as if invaded by a strong new power Mark cried out: "It's all bloody nonsense, and I'm damned if I do any such thing!" Through all his encrusted secularity, ambition, ignorance, and technocratic dreams there emerged sufficient courage to rebel. And while he was far from understanding it all—that Cross had again conquered.[17]

But we cannot stop with the Cross. On any test, the empty tomb is silent evidence that evil had had its one great hour of ruin.

> The pow'rs of death have done their worst,
> But Christ their legions hath dispersed;
> Let shouts of holy joy outburst, Alleluia! [18]

Calvary, then, is seen as the exposure of very God Incarnate to the worst strategy of evil. But through death and the resurrection, there is opened "the door between two worlds."

In the light of the resurrection, therefore, Calvary becomes intelligible. The Cross is not to be understood as an accident in an otherwise orderly world. It is not merely the expression of the abysmal depth of human hate. It is more than the convergence of historic events until Christ died as a martyr. In some peculiar sense we concur with Simon Peter's judgment before the enemies of the faith:

> This Man, Who was put into your power by the predetermined plan and foreknowledge of God, you nailed up and murdered, and you used for your purpose men without the Law! But God would not allow the bitter pains of death to touch Him. He raised Him to life again—and indeed there was nothing by which death could hold such a Man.
>
> *Acts 2:23f*

---

[17] C. S. Lewis, *That Hideous Strength* (London: The Bodley Head, Ltd., 1945), pp. 414ff.
[18] The Methodist Hymnal, No. 156.

I am more and more impressed by a certain insight that in the Cross there is the dramatic encounter of God and Evil. By its very nature Evil is divisive, solitary, alone,—always against, never for. Being basically discreative and destructive, it always disintegrates as it ruins. It can tolerate no other. Dante saw this and expressed it pictorially in the vision of Satan isolated at the lowest depth of Inferno frozen immobile in a cake of ice.[19] This discreative aloneness is dramatized in the meeting of Christ and Evil. In His early ministry He was the honored hero. Later, as He spoke of His coming sufferings, His popularity began to wane. "As a consequence of this, many of His disciples withdrew and no longer followed Him." (John 6:66) Then in the Upper Room there were the Twelve, but soon only Eleven. Out into the Garden eight were left at the gate and four serious-minded figures entered the darkness. But three of them were left behind, subsequently to sleep, while "he walked on a little way and fell on his face and prayed." (Matthew 26:39) But the utter penetration into the hidden evil of this solitary aloneness, this demonic destructiveness, came in the Cry of Dereliction: "My God, My God, why hast thou forsaken me?" (Mark 15:34, Matthew 27:46, RSV) To soften the grim note of this cry by suggesting that it is only a memory of the Psalmist's lament, or otherwise to minimize the obvious stark and dramatic intention of the Gospel, is completely to miss the meaning of this event. I am persuaded, if we are at all to retain a valid insight into the Divine initiative in Christ's coming into history, we must likewise see in this experience the redemptive intention of God to plumb the very depths of hell itself. There is no iniquitous crevice in this universe into which God has not thrust Himself. This truth has led Stewart to speak of "Love Incarnate taking upon itself the very worst that suffering and evil can do. . . God going into action once for all against the powers of darkness,

---

[19] See: Dante, *Inferno,* Canto, xxxiv.

Christ reigning from the deadly tree, and making His victory there the pledge and the assurance for all the sons of men." [20] Thus, Stewart can appeal to those who preach the Gospel.

> Let no one, listening to your preaching, have any doubt that when we Christians say that the dark demonic powers which leave their dreadful trail of devastation across the world are ultimately less powerful than Jesus, we really mean it—just as the early disciples meant it when they declared that Christ had raided the realm of Satan and broken the fast-bound chains of hell.[21]

In asserting that He personally penetrated into that destructive aloneness, we can assert it meant the descent into Hell, out on the other side of death holding in His hands the "keys of Death and the Grave." (Rev. 1:18) This means that at those places where life is most baffling, God has not simply spoken His last word, He has lived it out both within and beyond the boundaries of human history. It means there is no place in the universe beyond the range of His love. And while, through editorial accident, or deliberate purpose, the term "He descended into hell," was omitted from the American Methodist formulation of the Apostles' Creed—it still expresses this note of divine victory in the resurrection—victory where evil was most entrenched, those "spiritual agents from the very headquarters of evil." (Ephesians 6:12)

THE INCENTIVE FOR EVANGELISM

What to preach? To have asked this of a group of frightened nobodies in a secret upper room in Jerusalem, "with the doors locked for fear of the Jews," (John 20:19) would have seemed ridiculous. But soon this was the group to set upon the task to

---

[20] James S. Stewart, *Heralds of God* (New York: Charles Scribner's Sons, 1946), p. 78.
[21] *Ibid.*, p. 85.

turn the world upside down by proclaiming Christ was alive!

We must not forget the church moved out from behind closed doors with the message of the Risen Lord—not first of all with the Sermon on the Mount. It is not an accident that the sermons in the Book of Acts have as their theme, the Resurrection. It is no accident that every book of the New Testament presupposes the Risen Lord. Nor is it by chance that the focal center of the life of the early Church was the supreme confidence that He who had been crucified and buried stood among His followers to reconstitute them as the people of God. This was at once both the glory and offense of early preaching. People either believed or scoffed.

One thing which gave impetus to their evangelism was that the resurrection was a complete surprise. If there was one thing even those closest to Him did not expect—it was the resurrection. When He appeared He was not recognized; He had difficulty persuading them that He was alive.

What are the facts? Within a few weeks of the Crucifixion, and in the presence of those who had seen Christ die, and knew His tomb, He was publicly proclaimed as raised by God from His cursed and excommunicate death. More—He was being proclaimed as the Messiah of Israel, the Lord of all men. More—the disciples were witnesses to this divine event. More—anyone could now validate His Lordship for himself by a surrender of faith.

I am aware that divergent attempts have been made to interpret the fact of the resurrection. It has been set forth as a flesh-blood-bones existence. But this is essentially a restoration, a reanimation, the return to precisely the same kind of existence as Christ had prior to Calvary, and this is not New Testament resurrection. It has also been understood as mere spiritual survival, simply a continuance of the psyche after the death of the body. In some quarters today the tendency is to regard it mythologically. Resurrection is seen as a device to declare the resurrection faith which came to possess the

Church. It is said it is not important whether or not it happened. What is important is whether the spiritual truth of its proclamation comes to possess the believers.

For my part, I am persuaded, all data considered, we must retain the idea of the empty tomb. It is alleged that Paul did not know it. I believe this to be an error. After a careful study of every reference of Paul to the resurrection, I cannot escape the conviction that he was persuaded that He who had been crucified and buried had been raised from the tomb. As Hunter says: " 'Died, buried, raised'—the words are unintelligible unless they mean that what was buried was raised." [22] Thus Paul, in the sermon in Antioch in Pisidia, contrasts the death of Christ with that of David. Speaking of David, Paul says: "He did in fact 'see corruption,' but this Man Whom God raised never saw corruption!" (Acts 13:36f) Richardson is emphatic in his assertion that "it is exceedingly unlikely that St. Paul would have countenanced any notion of Christ's resurrection other than that of a physical resurrection in the sense of the narratives of the Empty Tomb." Thus, in his view, the Empty Tomb on Easter Morning is a part of the original tradition of the resurrection.[23] A similar interpretation is given by Canon Turner: as a firm basis for the "major miracles" in the transformations which took place in the lives of the disciples, as well as in the lives of all subsequent followers, Turner concludes: "Some objective ground in historical fact is required to account for these facts. Theories of pious mistake, fraud or hallucination cannot afford a satisfactory explanation. That given by the Apostolic Christians is still by far the most satisfactory." [24] And I am happy to concur with the conclusion by Bishop Lesslie Newbigin: "If the body of Jesus had remained in the tomb to moulder like any other human corpse, the dis-

---

[22] Hunter, *The Work and Words of Jesus, op. cit.,* p. 124.
[23] Richardson, *op. cit.,* pp. 196f.
[24] H. E. W. Turner, "The Resurrection," *Expository Times* (September, 1957), p. 371.

ciples would never have returned to Jerusalem, there would have been no Pentecost, no Christian preaching, and no Christian faith. Jesus would have been only another martyr." [25] This seems to be precisely what Paul is saying in I Corinthians 15:12f.

To speak of the Empty Tomb raises the question of what happened to the "body" of Christ. First, it should be said that this question confronts every interpretation of the Resurrection. Resuscitation requires that we ask: Did the "body" finally come to death as do all men? If it were stolen, then it must have been disposed of or discarded in some manner. It seems incredible that on the strength of such a pious fraud the disciples received the strength to evangelize the world and to die the death of martyrs, with none of them ever betraying the secret. Klausner speaks here with a Christian voice: "The nineteen hundred years' faith of millions is not founded on deception." [26] Was it merely a "spiritual" survival? Then, did the body still remain disintegrating in the tomb—all the while the church proclaimed that He was alive? We must agree with Cullmann: "Christian faith proclaims ... He arose *with* body and soul after He was fully and really dead." [27] Thus, to say anything about the "nature" of the Resurrection is not a requirement only of those who affirm an Empty Tomb. The disposal of the body is inescapable if we are to follow the New Testament claim that God's re-creative act emptied Joseph's tomb.

What can be said? For one thing, it would appear that the resurrection-body was sufficiently different for Christ not always to be readily recognized. We cannot think that Mary's reference to Him as the gardener and the failure of the Emmaus

---

25 Lesslie Newbigin, *Sin and Salvation* (Philadelphia: The Westminster Press, 1957), p. 90.
26 Joseph Klausner, *Jesus of Nazareth* (London: George Allen & Unwin, Ltd.; New York: The Macmillan Company, 1925), p. 359.
27 Oscar Cullmann, *Immortality of the Soul or Resurrection of the Dead?* (New York: The Macmillan Company, 1958), p. 38.

travelers to recognize their Companion of the Way were due solely to their inner confusion and unbelief. We may confidently believe that the resurrection of the body of Jesus effected such a change that He was not immediately known. (See John 20:15, Luke 24:16, 37, Matthew 28:17, John 20:25)

Also, one purpose of His appearances was to persuade His followers that He was alive. The Empty Tomb alone could not do that. Thus we may assume that He accommodated His Risen Self to their needs—as the evidence that He was alive. Richard R. Niebuhr's interpretation is that the purpose of these appearances was to identify this Risen Jesus in the memory of the disciples as the One with whom they had lived so intimately prior to Calvary. There is emphasis even on corporeality "insofar as it is the medium of recognition." Thus he claims that these appearances "must be accorded the status of historical independence and tangibility." [28]

This identification and recognition of the Risen Jesus with Him who had been crucified was essential both as historical fact and as present proclamation. Possibly Jesus' disclosure to Thomas is the best illustration of a time of transition from their dependence upon His earthly presence to their faith in Him as Victorious Lord—in preparation for the historical disappearance. After Thomas' confession of faith: "My Lord and My God" (John 20:28) Jesus said: "Is it because you have seen me that you believe? Happy are those who have never seen me and yet have believed!" (John 20:29) Thus the Risen Body was the expression of His Risen Self in a manner commensurate with His purpose to identify Himself and to seek to lead them to faith in His "spiritual body," that sort of existence consonant with the glorified life. "The whole period of the forty days represents a kind of half-way house, a time of accommodation or weaning of the disciples from the fellow-

---

[28] Richard R. Niebuhr, *Resurrection and Historical Reason* (New York: Charles Scribner's Sons, 1957), pp. 173, 175.

ship of sight and touch to new forms through the Spirit in the Church." [29]

Thus, when the church was thrust out into pagan society to proclaim its Gospel, it was a Gospel with the resurrection-event at the center. It was nothing so shallow as the claim that a man had survived death. It was far more than the growing consciousness that, in some strange manner the followers could not describe, He was spiritually present with them. It was the declaration that something had happened—that God has raised Him from the dead. As Kee has tersely put it: "It is meaningless to speak of the Easter faith as 'faith in the risen Lord' if the Lord never was raised." [30] This was "past history"; but it was also present event.

Both this past history and this present event must be more than an academic affirmation. It means that in every activity in the ministry of the kingdom there is the promise and presence of His own Glorious Living Self. This certainty of His Risen Presence was vividly brought home to me one Easter Sabbath when I was in the pastorate. Before morning worship a parishioner, who had been reared in the tradition of the Greek Orthodox faith, greeted me with the words: "Christ is Risen!" Into those words were poured centuries of meaning in this Eastern Christian greeting. And my western soul responded, meaningfully and feelingly, "He is Risen, Indeed!" This was the evangelical witness—within the fellowship of Christ's church.

LIFE WITHIN THE KINGDOM

The cynic has said we Americans should revise the promise of Our Lord to read: "Where two or three are gathered together, there will be a president, vice-president, and secretary-

---

[29] Turner, *op. cit.*, p. 371.
[30] Kee, *op. cit.*, p. 169.

treasurer." But this fellowship within the kingdom has a more profound dimension. "For where two or three are gathered together in my name, there am I in the midst of them." (Matthew 18:20, KJV) Is this presence a mere memory? Is it only symbol? Is it a vague sense of the "spiritual"? Or is it the embodiment of the dynamic life of God Himself in constituting the Church as the new people of God?

Some of the most vivid expressions in the New Testament pertain to this life within the kingdom: "My present life is not that of the old 'I,' but the living Christ within me." (Galatians 2:20) "God, who is rich in mercy, because of the great love he had for us, gave us life together with Christ." (Ephesians 2:5) "That Christ may actually live in your hearts by your faith." (Ephesians 3:17) Just as in baptism we have shared in His death, in Him we may share "the miracle of rising again to new life." (Colossians 2:13) Thus that "same divine energy which was demonstrated in Christ when He [God] raised Him from the dead" is available for every person. (Ephesians 1:19f) "Nevertheless once the Spirit of Him who raised Jesus from the dead lives within you He will, by that same Spirit, bring to your whole being new strength and vitality." (Romans 8:11)

The resurrection-life is to be understood as a new creation. It is a fresh beginning, the inauguration of a new epoch in God's purpose to constitute a New Israel. This New Israel is called a " 'chosen generation,' His 'royal priesthood,' His 'holy nation,' His 'peculiar people'—all the old titles of God's people now belong to you." (I Peter 2:9) This is what is meant by our privileged participation in the saving acts of God; in the death and resurrection of Jesus Christ. "When a man takes his stand within the community of the New Covenant, the cross and the resurrection become 'present' for him, just as they were present for the original eyewitnesses." [31]

---

[31] *Ibid.,* p. 172.

Biblical scholars are right in urging that one of the most valid witnesses to the resurrection is the church, the fellowship of believers. In a sense the idea of the *koinonia* (the fellowship of believers in the Risen Lord) may express the church as the "eschatological community" even more adequately than the more common New Testament term for the church, *ecclesia.* For, while the church was an assembly called out and a community called together, it was even more truly a fellowship which shared in the very life of the Risen Lord. It was the resurrection which shifted the sacred day of the Christians from the Jewish Sabbath to the Lord's Day, the Day of Resurrection.[32] As they met for worship their joy was expressed in "psalms and hymns and spiritual songs." (Ephesians 5:19) But it was the resurrection-faith which inspired these hymns as praise to the Risen Lord.[33] Their prayers were not only offered in the name of Jesus but, as has been shown, they were addressed to Him, that is, "Maranatha," "Our Lord, come!" (I Corinthians 16:22, RSV), and "Amen, come, Lord Jesus!" (Revelation 22:20) These, along with the prayer of the dying Stephen, indicate not only the desire of the Christians for their Lord to return, but the sense that He was presently alive, approachable in prayer, and alert to receive the worship of His Church. Also, one of the most definitive modes of worship

---

[32] See: H. Riesenfeld, "Sabbat et Jour du Seigneur," in *New Testament Essays,* edited by A. J. B. Higgins (Manchester University Press, 1959), especially: pp. 210f.

Is there any special significance to the construction of Matthew's report of the resurrection in 28:1:

> Does this say, literally, "At the end of the Sabbaths, toward the dawn of the first of the Sabbaths—"? And is it possible that this means, in the light of Matthew's Hebrew orientation, a claim that the old Sabbaths had now ended and the new Sabbaths had begun in the Resurrection event which inaugurated the Lord's Day?

[33] Various scholars have sought to identify elements of Christian hymns in the New Testament, as for example, John 1:1-14; Ephesians 5:14; I Timothy 3:16; 6:15f; II Timothy 2:11-13; James 1:17; Revelation 4:11; 5:9f; 12f; 11:17f; 15:3f. In the light of the total New Testament faith, it is not difficult to conclude that the Risen Lord is the inspiration for this singing witness.

was participation in the Holy Eucharist. The term itself, the "giving of thanks," was not mere gratitude that Christ had died for His Church, but also that He was alive and Present in its worship. As for the Scriptures used in the church, the thesis of our study seeks to show that in the kerygma, the irreducible core of the New Testament, the Resurrection was central.

If the Church of the mid-twentieth century could only become possessed by fellowship with the Living Lord as was the early Christian community! That strange phenomenon which fused a group of timid and frightened nobodies into an invincible band of witnesses to the Risen Christ: this was sheer miracle! The Apocalypse shows the Church victorious, though persecuted, standing over against the demonic elements of the Roman Empire—the symbol of Evil in history. What was the secret of survival, even of conquest? Devotion to the Slain Lamb, now the Lamb on the Throne, alive forevermore! This is metaphor, of course; but metaphor which speaks of something which actually happened—and continues to happen! The metaphor is simply the inadequate language of man used to express in human speech the work of God. This is the danger in the current emphasis upon de-mythologization: that a wedge be driven between the kerygma and the events which gave rise to the kerygma in the first place. Such apologetic tends toward a needless historical scepticism. For example, one can agree with Professor Carl Michalson that preaching "recreates the resurrection" in the sense that it "is always evoking the either/or decision between life and death which is precipitated in the living Lordship of the resurrected one." [34] Yet why should this writer appear to find it so necessary to castigate those who claim that in the proclamation of the resurrection as a contemporary event one is obliged to discount the fact that it

---

[34] Carl Michalson, "The Reality of the Resurrection," *The Drew Gateway* (Spring, 1959), volume xxix, Number 3, pp. 180f.

actually happened in history? Is there any intrinsic reason why the resurrection of Jesus Christ from the dead might not be understood both as the divine victory in a specific historical situation and also as the confrontation of men of every age, from that day to this, in their present religious experience?

If by saying that "The resurrection itself is not an event of past history" Bultmann means that it cannot be accounted for in terms of human antecedents, that is, in the normal manner of finding cause-and-effect within human history alone—this may be allowed. But if he means that the resurrection is not an event *in* past history, this is utterly unacceptable. And when he says "the historical problem is scarcely relevant to Christian belief in the resurrection," [35] he has taken a long step toward an eventual destruction of the resurrection-faith which he is so anxious to preserve. I for one fail to see why a confidence in the occurrence of an event in the past, admittedly an event of God's own doing, need interfere in the slightest with a vigorous claim to a present encounter with the Risen Lord.

In fairness to Bultmann, there is evident ambivalence, even ambiguity, in his view of the "historicity" of Jesus. For example, he can say: "The resurrection itself is not an event of past history." "The historical problem is scarcely relevant to Christian belief in the resurrection." [36] "An historical fact which involves a resurrection from the deed is utterly inconceivable!" [37] And perhaps his most famous claim is that we "can now know almost nothing concerning the life and personality of Jesus." [38] But at the same time, Bultmann claims that Jesus "is also a concrete figure of history" and in Him we have "a unique combination of history and myth." [39] Yet "the death of Christ . . . is not a 'historical event' to which one

---

[35] Bultmann, *Kerygma and Myth, op. cit.*, p. 42.

[36] *Ibid.*, p. 42.

[37] *Ibid.*, p. 39.

[38] Rudolf Bultmann, *Jesus and the Word* (New York: Charles Scribner's Sons, 1934, 1958), p. 8.

[39] Bultmann, *Kerygma and Myth,* op. cit., p. 34.

may look back as one may to the story of Moses. *The new people of God* has no real history, for it is the community of the
end-time, an eschatological phenomenon." [40] Thus "the figure
of Jesus cannot be understood simply from his context in
human evolution or history ... his origin transcends both
history and nature." [41] But again he argues that the cross is
"no mere mythical event, but a permanent historical fact origi-
nating in the past historical event which is the crucifixion of
Jesus." [42] At the same time "the meaning of the cross is not
disclosed from the life of Jesus as a figure of past history." [43]
"What God has done in Jesus Christ is not an historical fact
which is capable of historical proof. The objectifying historian
as such cannot see that an historical person (Jesus of Nazareth)
is the eternal Logos, the Word."

> That is the real paradox. Jesus is a human, historical person from
> Nazareth in Galilee. His work and destiny happened within world-
> history and as such come under the scrutiny of the historian who
> can understand them as part of the nexus of history. Nevertheless,
> such detached historical inquiry cannot become aware of what God
> has wrought in Christ, that is, of the eschatological event.[44]

Bultmann insists that "the cross and the resurrection form an
inseparable unity." [45]

What conclusions may we draw from these representative
sayings of Bultmann?

1. The Person, Jesus of Nazareth, while truly a human
being within history was also "at the same time the pre-existent
Son of God." [46] Thus, while the cross was an historical event,

40 Bultmann, *History and Eschatology*, *op. cit.*, p. 36.
41 Bultmann, *Kerygma and Myth*, op. cit., p. 35.
42 *Ibid.*, p. 37.
43 *Ibid.*, p. 38.
44 Bultmann, *Jesus Christ and Mythology*, op. cit., p. 80.
45 Bultmann, *Kerygma and Myth*, op. cit., p. 38.
46 *Ibid.*, p. 34.

He who died on it cannot be accounted for by purely historical antecedents.

2. At the same time, Bultmann insists that the cross and resurrection "form an inseparable unity." [47] Yet his insistence upon the nonhistorical character of the resurrection requires that we see in both cross and resurrection more than mere historical cause-and-effect. With this we agree. Their true significance cannot be evaluated by scientific objectivity.

3. When he argues that the death and resurrection of Christ have an existential meaning in every age, we concur, since "in the preaching of the Christian Church the eschatological event will ever again become present and does become present ever and again in faith." [48]

4. But it is when he severs the resurrection from any historical reference, seeking to regard it only in terms of the present encounter, that Bultmann takes his stand with those who would evacuate from the Christian faith everything which does not pass muster with a scientific view of the world as presently understood. And to date he has not succeeded in justifying himself before his critics. For example, there is sufficient discernment in the following evaluations to raise the question whether or not Bultmann really has a valid doctrine of Jesus in relation to history. First, Ian Henderson says:

> There must have been something about the actual Jesus at the time at which He was on earth, to make the New Testament witnesses summon men to decide for or against Him.... And if it is so, the historical facts about Jesus, and the mythological element in His life cannot have quite the subordinate role that Bultmann allots to them.[49]

---

[47] *Ibid.*, p. 38.

[48] Bultmann, *History and Eschatology, op. cit.*, p. 151.

[49] Ian Henderson, *Myth in the New Testament*, Studies in Biblical Theology No. 7 (London: SCM Press, Ltd., 1952. Distributed in U.S.A. by Alec R. Allenson, Naperville, Ill.), p. 49.

And Julius Schniewind asks:

> Do not Bultmann's disregard of the uniqueness and finality of Jesus
> and his interpretation of the event of Christ in terms of 'historic
> existence' betray him into reducing the Christological events to the
> levels of symbols or stimuli to devotion? [50]

Geraint V. Jones substantially answers Schniewind's question in the affirmative:

> Ultimately the existential encounter between the ever-contemporary
> Cross and the Christian to the exclusion of the 'historical' Jesus must
> lead to a kind of mysticism without factual content.[51]

Thielicke finds in this historical scepticism serious implication for the significance of Jesus: when the event of Jesus is
limited to a particular understanding of human life per se,
being basically meaningful only for human consciousness:
"The implication is that it would be nearer the truth to say:
'The Word did not become flesh.' . . . The status accorded by
Bultmann to the event in revelation would appear to be essentially indirect and negative." [52]

Finally, exhibiting a bit of professorial sarcasm, Robert E.
Cushman says: "It might be feasible once more to consider
the possibility that an 'act of God' could occur in God's own
world." [53]

With some justification, I feel, therefore, that Stewart has
spoken out most effectively against this historical scepticism.
And though his words are quite familiar, they should be
quoted in full:

---

[50] Schniewind, *Kerygma and Myth, op. cit.,* p. 74.

[51] Geraint V. Jones, *Christology and Myth in the New Testament* (London:
George Allen & Unwin, Ltd., 1956), p. 42.

[52] Helmut Thielicke, *Kerygma and Myth, op. cit.,* p. 148.

[53] Robert E. Cushman, "Is the Incarnation a Symbol?" *Theology Today*
(July, 1958), p. 182. (Printed with permission of *Theology Today*.)

But when the argument goes on to maintain that the New Testament has to be 'de-mythologized' before its Resurrection proclamation can be stated in existential terms, and that *what we call the outer history of our redemption has to be stripped off as an external shell before we can reach the kernel of truth,* then we have to retort that this is making the Resurrection mean something radically different from what those who first celebrated it knew it to be: a bleak and depressing prospect indeed for modern evangelism. The de-mythologizing school is perhaps not so modern as is generally supposed. Certainly some of its manifestations bear a curious resemblance to elements in ancient gnosticism. And what some present-day theologies do not understand is this—that the docetic tendency which they themselves would disown as heresy when it touches the Cross cannot suddenly become respectable as an interpretation of the Resurrection.[54]

Is it possible that those very elements which are claimed must be peeled away as myth constitute an indispensable purpose of God to vindicate the resurrection within their existential situation? For example, consider the several experiences of the disciples and the Risen Lord in the handling of food, namely: in the Emmaus Home, by the seaside, and among the frightened group at Jerusalem (Upper Room?). The important thing is not the broken bread, nor the bits of broiled fish: the important thing is that, just as they had known Him most intimately in the commonplace experiences of the sacrament of eating together, so too His Glorified and Risen Presence would continue to be with them in the routine day-by-day struggles.

At any rate, this is what happened: as the early followers moved away from the first flush of the resurrection-event the glow of His victorious Presence went with them. It was life within the kingdom. They were not to argue about a dead person but to be heralds of an encounter with a living pres-

---

[54] Stewart, *A Faith to Proclaim* (New York: Charles Scribner's Sons, 1953), pp. 108f. [Italics mine]

ence.[55] They were not to tell men about Jesus; they were to introduce men to Him.

The theology of the kerygma proclaims that this encounter with the Risen Lord is the most momentous experience for any person, for the church. "If you are then 'risen' with Christ, reach out for the highest gifts of Heaven, where your Master reigns in power." (Colossians 3:1) "Just as He was raised from the dead by that splendid revelation of the Father's power so we too might rise to life on a new plane altogether." (Romans 6:4)

I suppose the witness of Paul in the classical kerygmatic passage pertaining to the resurrection qualifies him to claim an encounter with the Risen Lord. ". . . and last of all, as if to one born abnormally late, He appeared to me!" (I Corinthians 15:8) Some years ago, preaching at an Easter Sunrise service, I was using this as the text for the message: "The Final Evidence of the Living Christ." The appeal was quite simple: the encouragement to believe that however meaningful were the events of the first Easter, we too can validate this divine deed of victory this morning, this hour, this moment. It was the offer, so daring I could never claim it was my own; it was on God's own authority: that any person, through personal surrender and faith in the Risen Lord, could have a meeting with Him no less meaningful than Mary Magdalene, the travelers to Emmaus, the disciples in the Upper Room, or Paul on the Damascus Road! The service being over, a bright little lady came up to me and said quietly: "Yes, I know what you mean! He is that real to me this morning. I'm a Catholic, on my way to Mass; I just wanted to tell you I've met the Risen Lord!"

For many years I have used the lines of John Masefield from *The Trial of Jesus* in preaching at Easter. Procula, the wife of Pontius Pilate, and Longinus, a centurion, are talking:

---

[55] See: Barclay, *op. cit.,* p. 115.

Procula: What do you think the man believed, Centurion?

Longinus: He believed that He was God, they say.

Pro: What do you think of that claim?

Lon: If a man believes anything up to the point of dying on the cross for it, He will find others to believe it.

Pro: Do you believe it?

Lon: He was a fine fellow, My Lady, not past middle age. And he was all alone and defied all the Jews and all the Romans, and, when we had done with Him, He was a poor broken-down thing, dead on the cross.

Pro: Do you think He is dead?

Lon: No, Lady, I don't.

Pro: Then, where is He?

Lon: Let loose in the world, Lady, where neither Roman nor Jew can stop His truth. *(Trumpet blows)*

That's for the setting of the watch, Lady.

Pro: Good-night, Centurion. (Longinus *goes. Right*)

Let loose in the dark night, with no friend; alone.[56]

But Procula: Do you know? "Let loose in the world"? Yes. "A dark night"? Yes. "Neither Roman nor Jew can stop His truth"? Yes. But: "With no friend; alone"? No, a thousand times "No." For millions have met Him at "the door between two worlds"! They too have walked through that door by baptism into His death and out into life by the power of His resurrection. They already have experienced that life which is beyond decay.

---

[56] John Masefield, *The Trial of Jesus* (London: William Heinemann, Ltd.), Act III. Permission granted by The Society of Authors and Dr. John Masefield, O.M.

FIVE

The Incarnation
Of The Holy Spirit

This, the fourth element of the kerygma, seems more suited to the prayer room than to the lecture hall. It is more devotional than doctrinal. Yet we must have not only theological clarity but devotional power. An adequate understanding of "The Incarnation of the Holy Spirit" could provide both.

It is Dodd's thesis that the evidence of the power of the Risen Lord is the Holy Spirit in the life of the church. "The Holy Spirit in the church is the sign of Christ's present power and glory." [1] As Simon Peter could say of Jesus, "He has been raised to the right hand of God; He has received from the Father and poured out upon us the promised Holy Spirit— *that* is what you now see and hear." (Acts 2:33)

John Marsh supports the view that the kingdom is a

---

[1] Dodd, *Apostolic Preaching*, op. cit., p. 42.

present reality by referring to the events of Pentecost as "assurances that the last days have arrived." This era was inaugurated by the Messianic action of Jesus in history. And they "are now continuing in his activity through the outpoured Spirit." [2] Thus when the early Christian witnesses began to declare the kerygma they not only announced the presence of the Holy Spirit within the Christian fellowship, they themselves were dynamic centers of personality in which the Spirit had found a new incarnation. This new quality of life has been variously described, but no one has related it more vividly to the ministry of Jesus in the days of His flesh than the late H. Wheeler Robinson. He has used the term "the kenosis of the Spirit" to indicate "that God as Holy Spirit enters into a relation to human nature which is comparable with that of the Incarnation of the Son of God at a particular point of human history." [3]

At the time I began my ministry each candidate was required to write a series of doctrinal sermons. My friend prepared his on the Holy Spirit. After being examined by the committee, it was returned with the comment: "This is a good sermon on the power of God, but there isn't any Holy Spirit in it." This is a parable of our confusion. In fact, we are confronted by a paradox: on the one hand, the New Testament makes an emphatic witness that the original Christians possessed a dynamic equal to any demand, while on the other hand, we who are their successors suffer from a paralyzing vagueness regarding the ministry of the Holy Spirit. This is serious as doctrinal obscurity. It becomes tragic when it betrays an inner emptiness of soul.

George S. Hendry has reminded us that Protestantism has

---

[2] John Marsh, *The Fulness of Time* (New York: Harper & Brothers, 1952), p. 122.

[3] H. Wheeler Robinson, *Redemption and Revelation* (New York: Harper & Brothers, 1942), p. 290.

been so preoccupied with the historical work of Christ that it has been relatively indifferent to the doctrines of the Spirit and the church.[4] May there be some specific reasons for this neglect?

For one thing, *an excessive emphasis upon divine immanence precludes a clear understanding of the Holy Spirit.* In 1902 George A. Coe said: "Theology has begun the twentieth century committed to the doctrine of the immanence of God." [5] God, man, and the world were regarded as one vast continuity. The doctrine that the life of God permeated all things was strikingly similar to pantheism. God in contrast to the world, over against the world, as "totally other" was rejected. The world process was seen as one organic and developing whole— with God substantially a prisoner within it. The revolution brought by Dialectical Theology had not yet come.

Likewise, *a resurgence of mysticism has tended to minimize or reject Trinitarian religion,* and with it any clear witness to the Holy Spirit. Since this total understanding of God is in terms of Spirit, there is no need for a special emphasis upon the Spirit. God as spiritual exhausts the concept of the divine. A doctrine of God as a life-force, in continuity as a divine life and the subconscious life of man, which is sought through the mystical disciplines, needs no idea of the Trinity. We might even say: God as spiritual almost comes to be the enemy of God as Holy Spirit. Even the most orthodox churches have felt the impact of this unitarian mood.

Also, *a sectarian appeal has doubtless frightened some people.* If some people have given too little attention to the Holy Spirit, others have given too much. Ecstatic sects, claiming unusual revelations and experiences, have little appeal for

---

[4] George S. Hendry, *The Gospel of the Incarnation* (Philadelphia: The Westminster Press, 1958), pp. 23f.

[5] George Albert Coe, *The Religion of a Mature Mind* (New York: Fleming H. Revell Company, 1902), p. 219.

modern man trained in academic procedures. As E. Stanley Jones once said: "Pentecostalism has hurt Pentecost very badly." [6]

And again, *when religion is interpreted as moralistic endeavor,* the place of the Holy Spirit is usurped by human effort. The Holy Spirit is thought of almost as the higher side of the human faculties. Even when we are urged to follow Jesus as leader or admire Him as the embodiment of the religious ideal, the recreative ministry of the Holy Spirit is subordinate to a do-it-yourself religion.

At present, however, there is a new interest in the doctrine of the Holy Spirit. Among other reasons is the attempt to understand the meaning of "church." To use a term of Lesslie Newbigin, our ecumenical studies have brought us face to face with "the community of the Holy Spirit." [7] Newbigin speaks of the incompleteness of the "Catholic-Protestant debate," since in it there has been a serious neglect of the place of the Holy Spirit. Yet "in very truth it is the presence of the Holy Spirit which constitutes the Church." [8] Within the ecumenical fellowship this is the neglected note in our concern for unity. "What I have called the Pentecostal Christian has the New Testament on his side when he demands first of all of any body of so-called Christians, 'Do you have the Holy Spirit? For without that all your credal orthodoxy and all your historic succession avails you nothing.' " [9]

Our concern now for "The Incarnation of the Holy Spirit" will seek to do two things: (1) to learn how the church was prepared for this new invasion of divine life and (2) to look at some of the consequences of it.

---

[6] E. Stanley Jones, *The Christ of Every Road* (Nashville: Abingdon Press, 1930), p. 48.

[7] Newbigin, *The Household of God, op. cit.,* pp. 94f.

[8] *Ibid.,* p. 98.

[9] *Ibid.,* p. 101.

THE CHURCH IN PREPARATION

My phone rang one morning and a fellow minister asked where he might get information on the events between Easter and Pentecost. He had announced a series of sermons on experiences during these days, and now the calendar had caught up with him. Among other things I urged him not to omit the Emmaus Road experience. For a long time I have regarded this as a little transcript of how we all live—under the impulse to do the will of God, yet not sure how to do it. Luke tells of two of Jesus' followers on the road to a village called Emmaus: "While they were absorbed in their serious talk and discussion, Jesus Himself approached and walked along with them. . . . Then they said to each other, 'Weren't our hearts glowing while He was with us on the road, and when He made the Scriptures so plain to us?' " (Luke 24:15, 32)

Notice how the Christian lives at *the growing edge of both hope and despair.* "We were hoping"—"it's getting on for three days." (Luke 24:21) If I were attempting to make it academically respectable, I should say: This was the dialectic of despair. They had hoped; but He died. The women found the tomb empty; but they did not find Him. Mackay has called this experience "hours of gloom." Life had reached the twilight stage, a kind of theological parenthesis expressed as a mood of "quiet desperation." [10]

I have come to feel that one reason for the frequent anaemia of modern religious living is that we have not yet touched the bottom of desperation. We lack the burning sense of dread, of being cut off from all hope. We have not been thrust upon our own emptiness sufficiently to learn how helpless we are in rebuilding our own broken moral life. We are like the man in the crow's nest of the ship, tossed from side to side by the

---

[10] John A. Mackay, *A Preface to Christian Theology* (New York: The Macmillan Company, 1948), pp. 45f.

rolling of the waves, alternately suspended over the abyss on one side or the other.[11] Romantic optimists often object to the sentimentality of hymns of heaven, preferring, rather, the mood that this is God's good earth—we should enjoy it. But there is this irony: it is a preoccupation with *this* world which often leads to despair in our attempt to enjoy it. The Emmaus pilgrims were caught in a tension between hope and despair. Yet into this desperation came the Incarnation of the Holy Spirit.

The release from this sense of despair was the disclosure of God. "Jesus Himself approached and walked along with them." (Luke 24:15) There is no suggestion that anything they did created the experience. This must be seen as the direct intervention of God. Jesus turned them to their Scriptures to learn that God's messenger, His Anointed One, the Messiah, was the destined Sufferer. There is here an interesting Greek construction. As they were walking, they were throwing their doubts back and forth to each other. The last thing they ever dreamed might happen did happen: their dead Lord joined them on their journey. This experience was not a human creation; it was the act of God. It was so unexpected, and they were so unprepared. William Barclay includes an interesting poem in his discussion of this event:

> Sometimes, when everything goes wrong;
> When days are short and nights are long;
> When wash-day brings so dull a sky
> That not a single thing will dry.
> And when the kitchen chimney smokes,
> And when there's naught so "queer" as folks!
> When friends deplore my faded youth,
> And when the baby cuts a tooth.
> While John, the baby last but one,
> Clings round my skirts till day is done;

---

[11] See: S. Kierkegaard, *The Concept of Dread* (Princeton: Princeton University Press, 1944), p. 55.

And fat, good-tempered Jane is glum,
And butcher's man forgets to come.
Sometimes I say on days like these,
I get a sudden gleam of bliss.
Not on some sunny day of ease,
He'll come ... but on a day like this! [12]

After all is said about the Resurrection, it finally rests upon the self-disclosure of God in our lives. And the temptation is ever with us to adapt the Risen Lord in all sorts of ways. In my college days He was hailed almost in the image of the successful business executive. Later some people saw Him as a sentimental dreamer. Others wanted to romanticize Him. Educators conspired to instrumentalize Him. Professional theologians sought to eschatologize Him, and now the current fashion of the learned world is to de-mythologize or existentialize Him. We are willing to do almost anything except to worship Him, and to say: "My Lord and My God!"

We are even tempted to exalt the Sermon on the Mount as if it were the total Christian message. It would be well if we got that far. The Sermon has revolutionary social implications. But it says next to nothing about Who proclaimed this message, why He came, what He did, the meaning of His death and resurrection. A former student, discouraged in his first parish, wrote quite dejectedly: "How can I get beyond merely teaching ethics to people who are already within the church? How can I get kerygma over to them?" It was into some such mood as this that there came the Incarnation of the Holy Spirit.

Again, notice *how personal and intimate was this presence of the Risen Lord.* "Weren't our hearts glowing while He was with us on the road—?" (Luke 24:32) Jesus did not argue His presence. He simply let the impact of His own victory over sin and death bear its own certitude. "They knew Him!" I'm

---

[12] William Barclay, *The Gospel of Luke* (Philadelphia: The Westminster Press, 1957), pp. 309f.

glad it was in a humble setting, at a simple meal, in a home, holding the loaf. This was truly a sacramental experience. How often He sanctifies the commonplace and makes it the channel of His glory.

And this experience of the Risen Lord made of the church a *worshipping and a witnessing community.* "They got to their feet without delay and turned back to Jerusalem. There they found the Eleven and their friends all together full of the news—'The Lord is really risen—He has appeared to Simon now.'" (Luke 24:33) Emmaus no longer seemed important. They had left the Holy City too soon. The place of tragedy was to be the scene of triumph—but they had gone. Now their steps turned again to the place where God had demonstrated life beyond the reach of death.

Where does one go after Calvary? The young people of the church asked me to speak for them the Sunday evening following Easter. And they provided the theme: "After Calvary—So What?" With all its implied cynicism, it is a good question. And the clue is found at Emmaus. Never again could those men be neutral. They were now part of the world Christian community. They had entered into the greatest enterprise ever to stir the souls of men. As it has been said: "Jesus promised His disciples that they would be completely fearless, absurdly happy, and in constant trouble." [13]

This seems to be a transcript of what Jesus was trying to get these timid, fearful, frustrated, confused men to see—and to experience. That strange ministry between the Opened Tomb and the Upper Room was the prelude to the Incarnation of the Holy Spirit.

---

[13] Paul R. Clifford, *The Mission of the Local Church* (London: SCM Press, Ltd., 1953), p. 81.

THE CONSEQUENCES OF
THE INCARNATION

Donald M. Baillie, in *God Was in Christ*, his definitive study of the mission of Jesus, has a section which he calls "The Legacy of the Incarnation." [14] The sequel to the Incarnation is to be understood as the ministry of the Risen and Glorified Lord. Baillie reminds us that the followers of Jesus must often have faced the question: "What can make up to us for the loss of the actual presence of Jesus on earth?" The answer was clear: it came from Pentecost, not as a mere memory, but as a divine Presence in the Person of the Holy Spirit. Those who were to live within the continuing Christian fellowship were to be at no disadvantage as compared with those who knew Him in Galilee. Just as a new divine event had taken place with Jesus as God manifest in the flesh, so a permanent and continuing event carries on His work. "The God who was incarnate in Christ is still present with us and in us through the Holy Spirit." [15]

What are some of the consequences of this continued ministry of Christ, understood within a full Trinitarian faith?

1. Whatever else the Incarnation of the Holy Spirit means, it provides our clearest insight into *the nature of the church*. We are now involved in discussions on "The unity we seek." It is so easy to become peripheral. A friend, while a student in Scotland, was on the staff of a cathedral where a new bishop was about to be enthroned. The occasion attracted ecclesiastical dignitaries from throughout Europe and the rest of the world. The long procession was most impressive. My friend told me, off the record, that the most difficult question troubling those

---

[14] Donald M. Baillie, *God Was in Christ* (New York: Charles Scribner's Sons, 1948), p. 151.
[15] *Ibid.*, pp. 153f.

in charge of arrangements was to decide who should precede whom in the procession. "Lord, give us priority in the Procession!"

Students of the ecumenical movement remember the advances made at Amsterdam. Three views of the church were proposed: the "catholic," with the emphasis upon continuity, historical traditions, the institutional life in terms of episcopacy. The "protestant" view was concerned with justification by faith, the position of the believer as priest before God, faith as God's gift to man, the preaching of the Word and the administration of the sacraments. These were adopted as valid. But there was also proposed a third interpretation, the *gathered* church, the church *assembled* for worship, the community of the Holy Spirit. It is interesting to note that this was rejected by high churchmen and free churchmen alike. But it was defended by Protestant Episcopal Bishop Angus Dun of Washington, D. C., on the ground that it conserved the idea of the presence of the Spirit in the life of the church. It is no secret that the rejection of this view had in it a large element of expediency; there were nervous tensions among various groups, in spite of their determination to "stay together."

I wonder if the price of such "unity" is too great? I believe the Ecumenical Movement must eventually bear witness that we need this emphasis upon the life of the Spirit as the secret of the unity of the church. Beyond all orders, all claims of succession, all concerns for sacraments, and all other authorities— is the Holy Spirit who permeates the life of the church—across all boundaries. E. Stanley Jones is so right when he urges that Jesus provided no successor to Himself except the Holy Spirit. To refer once again to Bishop Lesslie Newbigin, he concurs that it is often suggested in ecumenical studies that progress in unity may be found in a new understanding of the doctrine of the Holy Spirit. He then brings us up to the practical implications of this view by a disturbing question: "May it not be that the great Churches of the Catholic and Protestant traditions will have to be humble enough to receive it in fellowship with their brethren in the various groups of the Pentecostal type with whom at present they have scarcely any Christian fellowship at all?" [16]

The unity we seek, therefore, is in terms of the Holy Spirit within the life of the church. If we place the emphasis elsewhere, we turn to the marginal. If we place the emphasis here, all else is marginal. We are not dependent upon any one interpretation of the church as holding exclusive divine sanction. I doubtless betray my own naïveté here. But I honestly believe it is in proportion as we stress organization, ministries, orders, sacraments, institution, and ecclesiastical functions that we move further and further into division. The unity we achieve in this fashion is by compromise, coercion, or exclusiveness of any sort—episcopal, sacramental, mystical, evangelical, or any other—and it will only sow the seeds of greater disunity. I should go further and urge that unless there is a mutual recognition of orders, ministries, sacraments, governments, and polities, the unity of the church will be impossible. And the fault will lie not simply with the sect-type churches of the Pentecostal tradition (to use Newbigin's term) but with the rigid insistence upon some exclusive interpretation of the nature of the church—often in terms of succession.

A former student has left the church of his birth and rearing to enter one with a more sacramental ministry. The reason he gives is that his former church has no adequate concept of the church and ministry. He could not understand when I reminded him that the greatest bottleneck to unity has been in a communion which has been quite vocal about it—all the while holding in reserve a doctrine of the church regarded as so sacrosanct as to be beyond further examination. Actually, this is an aggravated example of sectarianism at its worst! To put it bluntly: any insistence that episcopacy *must* occupy a

---

16 Newbigin, *op. cit.,* p. 122.

definitive position in the ecumenical church betrays a grievous misunderstanding of the New Testament idea of the church's ministry.

The recent study by Hendrik Kraemer should require us to rethink this entire disposition to interpret the church in terms of its clerical character. I refer, of course, to *A Theology of the Laity*. [17] Professor Kraemer reminds us that quite early the church deviated from the New Testament understanding of the people of God as the "laos" to turn toward the "kleros" concept taken from the Graeco-Roman culture. The result was, the idea that the *whole* church as "a royal priesthood" became subordinate to the special function "of an organized, duly ordained clergy as a closed 'status' over against the 'laos,' the people." [18] Kraemer's position is so clear and unequivocal that it should be reported at length:

> The concentration on considerations of rights and validity, on ordinances and the observance of rites, on the different theological accounts of the mystery hidden in the Lord's meal as the appropriation of His atoning death, has done more in the course of history to conceal and obscure the Church than to manifest its true nature.... Moreover, the predominant concentration on these marks of the Church as the only essential ones has contributed enormously to the feeling amongst the laity of being objects and subjects in the Church. It artificially narrows our thinking on the Church, its being and purpose. It is the reason why the ecumenical discussion on the Church continues to centre around Ministry and Sacraments. This is too narrow.[19]

Reinhold Niebuhr echoes this judgment upon the church interpreted in terms of orders and sacraments. Such things belong to the realm of the historically contingent but "by

---

[17] Hendrik Kraemer, *A Theology of the Laity* (Philadelphia: The Westminster Press, 1958).

[18] *Ibid.,* pp. 50f.

[19] *Ibid.,* p. 125.

insisting that the basis of ecumenical unity must include both a common faith and a common 'order' " leads inevitably to further dividedness, and introduces "confusion into the ecumenical movements of the non-Roman churches." The same is true when the sacrament of the Lord's Supper is made the symbol of church unity in being administered "according to a particular 'order.' " [20]

From a somewhat different perspective the late T. W. Manson has raised the question of the validity of ministries. He points out that a rigid distinction within the New Testament between the episcopate and the presbyterate is not justified. As for succession, it could be forfeited only by apostasy, not even by death—since it "could not be transmitted to another." [21] And as for apostolicity, it belongs to the Church as Church, "not to any particular form of ministry." [22] Thus the "signs of the Apostle" are not found exclusively within any one church tradition. There is one essential ministry and that is the perpetual ministry of the Risen Lord.[23] All other ministries are derivative, functional, and dependent upon His ministry.[24] Thus, what difference does it make if a man is ordained by a bishop or presbytery? "So far as his qualification to minister is concerned, none whatever. If he has been called and equipped by Christ, all the bishops, presbyteries, and congregational meetings in the world cannot make him any more a minister than he already is." [25] This requires what we have been urging all the time—a full and frank mutual recognition of ministries— or the willingness to have none at all!

It is our claim that the Church understood in terms of the

---

[20] Reinhold Niebuhr, *The Nature and Destiny of Men,* vol. ii (New York: Charles Scribner's Sons, 1943), p. 225 and note.

[21] T. W. Manson, *The Church's Ministry* (London: Hodder & Stoughton Limited, 1948), pp. 51, 59, 86.

[22] *Ibid.,* p. 73.

[23] *Ibid.,* p. 76.

[24] *Ibid.,* p. 95.

[25] *Ibid.,* p. 97.

Incarnation of the Holy Spirit, will determine the doctrine of the ministry, not vice versa. The ministry is a gift of the Holy Spirit to the Church. And that gift may, and often does, extend to the laity as well as to the officially designated clergy. A friend of mine asked a bishop in India if Jesus would be permitted to preach in his church. The bishop was honest enough to say he could not permit Our Lord to do so since He obviously had not been properly ordained. This is the absurd logic of any interpretation of the church other than the high doctrine of church as the Body of Christ in which the Holy Spirit is Incarnate. And when He is so incarnate, diversities of ministries are relatively flexible and within the direct call of God upon the person.

2. Also the Incarnation of the Holy Spirit is a valid way to understand the church as *the extension of the Incarnation.* George S. Hendry has put the matter quite succinctly: "The extension of the incarnation then must be defined as the presence of the Spirit in the church; for the presence of the Spirit is the presence of Christ." [26] If we regard the coming of Our Lord as a sort of divine beachhead in human affairs, so the Incarnation of the Holy Spirit may be understood as the continuing conquest of history in His behalf. As in the "fulness of the times" God sent His Son, so in a further "fulness of the times" the Holy Spirit infused the divine life within the church. And the theological significance of this new dimension of life is evident in the work of the Holy Spirit to witness to Christ, to direct the church to proclaim the first Christian creed, "Jesus is Lord." (I Corinthians 12:3)

The church is called to move beyond a secondhand dependence upon the memory of Jesus to a firsthand witness of His risen life. God's involvement in human affairs, even to the penetration into the predicament of sin, did not end with the death of Christ. The redemptive power of His risen life

---

[26] Hendry, *op. cit.*, p. 159.

is to permeate the life of the church of all ages. As T. F. Torrance says: "The original event becomes event all over again through the power of the Spirit so that in *kerygma* a man encounters the living Christ, Christ crucified but risen." [27]

As in our previous discussion, it is the presence of the Spirit which safeguards the interpretation of the church as the "Extension of the Incarnation" from an exclusive institutional entity. Likewise, it is the ministry of the Spirit which assures the perpetuation of the Church as the redemptive ministry of Christ in history. As Cullmann puts it:

> The victory of Christ over sin and death has ushered in this reign of the Holy Spirit on earth. This reign still belongs to the present age, but to the end of this age, since the Holy Spirit which belongs to the coming age, is already at work in it. The conquered powers still possess a certain strength; sin and death have not been abolished, though they are irremediably doomed to destruction by the death and resurrection of Jesus Christ and the work of the Holy Spirit.[28]

3. This interpretation of the Incarnation of the Holy Spirit clarifies our *relation to all non-Christian religions.* The issue is acute: How to relate the Christian Gospel to the revived world religions, especially national religions, and still preserve the exclusiveness which defines the faith? Some years ago the simple confession of an old professor opened a little window for me into this problem. He said: "There is no human being who has not heard the voice of the Holy Ghost." [29]

God as Spirit has access to the inner life of all men. While we should hesitate to claim that it makes no difference what religion a man pursues, we do claim that God is not limited in His ministry to those who are officially Christian. The Holy

---

[27] T. F. Torrance, "A Study in New Testament Communication," *Scottish Journal of Theology* (September, 1950), p. 311.

[28] Cullmann, *The Early Church, op. cit.,* p. 156.

[29] Lynn Harold Hough, *The Theology of a Preacher* (New York: Eaton & Mains, 1912), p. 135.

Spirit is God pressing in upon every life to turn it from evil to goodness. God does not see people as Hindus, Buddhists, Muslims, Hebrews, or Christians. God sees people as people. Wherever men and women think, feel, struggle, desire, and search for the noblest life restless within their souls, there God is seeking again the Incarnation of Himself. This understanding of the Spirit is not the attempt to reaffirm the truth of the old doctrine of natural theology, but it is to restate it. It means that there are degrees or levels of revelation of God, that God is nowhere without His one witness. It means that all truth is God's truth—and every insight which every man has, or has ever had, comes from God. The astronomer, the mathematician, the physicist, the chemist, the sociologist, the psychologist, as well as the man of religion—all experience the effort of God to get His wisdom into the life of that man. It could even be said that God is struggling under all circumstances to extend the Incarnation of the Holy Spirit into the life of His people. H. Wheeler Robinson has pointed out that "the Old Testament is part of our Bible to remind us that the Spirit of God cannot be confined to the Christian Church." [30] But likewise, "the God of the Church is also the God of Nature and of History"; His constant activity as Spirit is "in the whole extra-ecclesiastical world." [31] In fact, if we are to take seriously the claim that God has not left Himself without witness anywhere in the world, must we not mean that wherever men have been impelled in the direction of righteousness and wisdom and justice, that this is the Spirit of God at work?

In Leonard Hodgson's illuminating series of Gifford Lectures he vividly shows how the Holy Spirit is involved in the revelation of all truth in man's history upon earth. He vigorously argues that the personal creative spirit of God is a more reasonable interpretation of the natural order than to view

---

[30] H. Wheeler Robinson, *The Christian Experience of the Holy Spirit* (London: Nisbet & Co., Ltd., 1928), p. 157.

[31] *Ibid.*, p. 157.

it as permeated by some vague spiritual force. Thus he claims
that the Holy Spirit is at work in what we are prone to refer
to as "the sub-human stages of the creative process." [32] "It
is by the Holy Spirit that grass grows and trees bring forth
leaves and flowers and fruit, that birds fly and fishes swim, that
engines turn and trains and cars and aeroplanes go on their
way." [33] This may be dismissed as poetic fancy, but it may not
be so dismissed if one takes seriously the claim that God is
the source of all truth and that every increase of human understanding of our world of things as well as persons is a measure
of divine disclosure. This is merely to affirm that all truth is
of a piece. There can be no pluralistic understanding of truth
in a theistic world. Thus Hodgson can say: "All human apprehension of truth is man receiving the self-revelation of God." [34]

Now if we can claim this from our knowledge of the natural
order, how much more when we apply this principle to persons. It is precisely because we believe God's Holy Spirit has
His certain status within the life of every man that we can
approach any man with the Gospel which is for all men.

4. Finally, it is the ministry of the Holy Spirit *to produce
the quality of sanctity within the Church.* Sainthood is often
associated with ancient piety. But it has about it an air of
mechanization by way of official sanctions by the hierarchy.
The possibility of sainthood is not popular within Protestantism. The resurgence of Reformation piety with its emphasis upon man being justified and sinful at the same time
(simul justus et peccator) substantially precludes any adequate
understanding of New Testament sanctity. This tendency in
Neo-Reformation thought is not surprising since, as R. Newton
Flew has reminded us, "Luther taught that sin was uncon-

---

[32] Leonard Hodgson, *For Faith and Freedom,* vol. ii (New York: Charles
Scribner's Sons; Oxford: Basil Blackwell, 1957), p. 106.

[33] *Ibid.,* p. 107.

[34] Leonard Hodgson, *For Faith and Freedom,* vol. i (New York: Charles Scribner's Sons; Oxford: Basil Blackwell, 1956), p. 115.

querable in this life," [35] and John Baillie says that "the main development of Reformation thought estimates very lightly the possibility of the acquisition of holiness during this present life." [36]

And Baillie, who cannot in any way be bracketed with the pietistic perfectionists, feels that the Reformation emphasis upon justification and assurance of forgiveness does tend to neglect the emphasis upon sanctification. He argues that a justification which does not issue in sanctification is no true justification at all. That is, if it is only a good tree which produces good fruit, then our persistent failure to become more holy should raise a question even concerning our reconciliation with God. And he refers to the "lesser Protestant sects" (including the Methodists!) who gave evangelical accent to the idea of sanctity. Baillie becomes almost Wesleyan when he follows through on this vision: "Of the few things I know, there is nothing that I know with a clearer and more immediate conviction than that I must not be *satisfied* with anything that is less than *perfect*." [37]

It is our claim that a proper appreciation of the Incarnation of the Holy Spirit will produce a new concern for saintliness in Christian living. We cannot take seriously the moral claims of Christ, "You are to be perfect, like your Heavenly Father," (Matthew 5:48), and read this to say: "You must be almost perfect—," or "You must be *partly* perfect—," or "You must be perfect *here and there, now and then—*."

But what might a new and fresh call to sanctity include as relevant for our time?

(a) For one thing, it will include a *life clean both within and without, in action and attitude.* Nothing less than this is worthy of the goal of any person committed to Christ. A Ger-

---

[35] R. Newton Flew, *The Idea of Perfection in Christian Theology* (London: Oxford University Press, 1934), p. 255.

[36] John Baillie, *Invitation to Pilgrimage* (London: Oxford University Press; New York: Charles Scribner's Sons, 1942), p. 71.

[37] *Ibid.,* p. 96.

man war bride, struggling with this new American language, prayed: "O God, *clean* me!" Her verb may have been wrong, but her concern was right! A whole cluster of New Testament terms points to this need for moral purity: purge, wash, cleanse, purify, sanctify. The doctrine is given classic expression in the Collect for Purity, derived from the Gregorian Sacramentary.

> Almighty God, unto whom all hearts be open, all desires known, and from whom no secrets are hid; Cleanse the thoughts of our hearts by the inspiration of thy Holy Spirit, that we may perfectly love thee, and worthily magnify thy holy Name; through Christ our Lord. Amen.

The Methodist, also, has ample scope to sing of this expectation.

> O for a heart to praise my God,
>   A heart from sin set free,
> A heart that always feels Thy blood
>   So freely shed for me.
> A heart in every thought renewed,
>   And full of love divine;
> Perfect, and right, and pure, and good,
>   A copy, Lord, of Thine!
>   *Charles Wesley* in *Methodist Hymnal* #370

> Refining fire, go through my heart,
>   Illuminate my soul;
> Scatter Thy life thro' every part,
>   And sanctify the whole.
>   *Charles Wesley* in *Methodist Hymnal* #371

(b) The saintly life is a *life of boundless love*. This is love without frontiers, geographical, ecclesiastical, cultural, or racial. I have heard numerous sermons pointing toward the holy life, but few based upon the famous thirteenth chapter of I Corinthians. Yet this is the classic appeal for love without boundaries:

This love of which I speak is slow to lose patience—it looks for a way of being constructive. It is not possessive: It is neither anxious to impress nor does it cherish inflated ideas of its own importance.

Love has good manners and does not pursue selfish advantage. It is not touchy. It does not keep account of evil or gloat over the wickedness of other people. On the contrary, it is glad with all good men when Truth prevails.

Love knows no limit to its endurance, no end to its trust, no fading of its hope; it can outlast anything. It is, in fact, the one thing that still stands when all else has fallen.

I Corinthians 13:4-8

(c) Sainthood also involves a *life of indescribable peace.* "Thou dost keep him in perfect peace, whose mind is stayed on thee, because he trusts in thee" is the affirmation of Isaiah 26:3 (RSV). This is vastly more profound than a shallow "peace of mind"; it is the "peace of God which transcends human understanding." (Philippians 4:7) I am persuaded it is the will of God for us to possess this sort of peace which can sing songs at the darkest midnight.

When I see a man like Martin Luther King, Jr. daily meet the bitterness of those who often profess the name of Christ, risk personal injury to himself and his family, endure constant harassment and denunciation by people in high places in church and in state, yet all the while quietly pursuing the path of refusing to strike back or returning hate for hate, this becomes a demonstration of that quality of peace which Our Lord had when confronted by His enemies. I am reminded of the East German pastor who, when faced with possible ejection from his church by Communist authorities, said: "I now see if they take from me my congregation in East Germany, they will give me another one in Siberia!"

(d) This is a *life of disciplined power.* It is pointed out that two permanent results of the coming of the Holy Spirit upon the church at Pentecost were purity and power—power within ordinary people now become extraordinary because possessed by a dynamic not their own. This was to be the continuing privilege of all who participate in the Christian community. Several years ago Anderson Scott interpreted this invasion of human personality by the Holy Spirit at Pentecost as "life of a new quality, life which quickened deeper levels of personality, and related men to one another and to God in a bond which neither death nor life could break." [38] I like to think of this spiritual reenforcement not as resembling the dangerous tumult of a river sweeping out of control over its banks, but rather as the quiet lake, held behind the dam, ready to plunge through the turbines to produce light and energy. At least it was such a disciplined power which came to the followers of Jesus when they took seriously His promise: "You are to be given power when the Holy Spirit has come to you." (Acts 1:8)

(e) The saintly life is a *life of social righteousness*. During the latter part of the last century a British Churchman said that the Methodists had permitted John Wesley's doctrine of Christian holiness, or sanctity, to remain static and unused without proper application to social situations. Though this charge may possibly be made against some of the sons of Wesley, it does not apply to John himself. The social evil of his day felt the impact of the Gospel proclaimed and practiced within the Wesleyan Societies: slavery, drunkenness, luxurious living, political corruption, poverty, all were cited for correction. Wesley himself established knitting guilds to enable poor women to make a living. He ministered to the dispossessed colliers of the land. He advocated stringent restrictions upon the gambling and wicked excesses of the rich while the poor people were underfed. He studied medicine and possibly established the first medical dispensary in Great Britain. And when Methodism has been loyal to her heritage, devotion to

---

[38] C. A. Anderson Scott, *The Fellowship of the Spirit* (London: James Clarke & Co., Ltd., 1921), p. 46.

the elimination of social evils has been integral to her Gospel. Anything which keeps persons from their best must be purged from the practices and policies of society.

Sitting in the office of a small college in England, where Methodist lay evangelists are trained, the Principal spoke to me of the history of the school. He said two things had been traditional in its purpose: earnest evangelism and Scriptural holiness. He then added: "We have now felt we must add a third—social righteousness." So it is: the Incarnation of the Holy Spirit is to motivate the followers of Christ to labor to correct poverty, illiteracy, hunger, disease, social drinking, colonialism, the exploitation of the poor, racial discrimination, and all causes of sin which infect society.

It is a tragedy of the first order that some of those who are most ardent in their earnestness for evangelism in America have been woefully deficient in sensing a proper responsibility in these areas. And, worst of all, some fundamentalist groups along with well-known churchmen have actually sought to preserve such wicked institutions as racial segregation.

(f) Finally, the saintly life can become a *life of contagious radiance*. This is where the theology of the Incarnation of the Holy Spirit becomes incarnation again in the moral excellence of personality. While theologians may find learned reasons to argue why sainthood is impossible in a fallen world, it is the witness of the simple saintly life which belies such speculations. It can be said of those of the mid-century as it was of those in the early church: "Verily, this is a new people, and there is something divine in the midst of them!" [39]

I think no one has expressed the meaning of this Incarnation of the Holy Spirit more adequately for me than E. Stanley Jones. He speaks of the Holy Spirit as "God in action." "He is

---

[39] Aristides, *Apology*, Chapter 16, *The Ante-Nicean Fathers*, vol. ix (New York: Charles Scribner's Sons, 1903), p. 278. See also: *Texts and Studies*, Ed. J. R. Harris and J. A. Robinson, Vol. 1, 1, Cambridge, 1891.

God where it counts—within us." And the contagious radiance is found in these words:

> A strange, sober joy went across that sad and decaying world—joy that goodness was here for the asking, that moral victory was possible now, that guilt could be lifted from the conscience stricken, that inner conflict could be resolved and inner unity found, that the total person could be heightened and a 'plus' added to one, and that a Fellowship of like-souled persons gave one a sense of *belonging*. It was Good News. And it worked." [40]

In the end, when confronted with the offer of the Incarnation of the Holy Spirit, the wise words of Leon Bloy haunt us: "There is but one sadness, and that is for us NOT to be SAINTS." [41]

---

[40] E. Stanley Jones, *The Way to Power and Poise* (Nashville: Abingdon Press, 1949), pp. 28f.

[41] Leon Bloy, *Pilgrim of the Absolute* (New York: Pantheon Books, 1947), p. 301.

SIX

Until He Comes!

According to Dodd, the fifth element in the kerygma is: "The Messianic Age will shortly reach its consummation in the return of Christ." [1] (See footnote, p. 3.) "Then He will send you Jesus, your long-heralded Christ, although for the time He must remain in Heaven until that universal Restoration of which God spoke in ancient times through all His Holy Prophets." (Acts 3:21) Dodd recognizes that this is the only reference to the Return of Christ in the early chapters of Acts, though it is stated in chapter ten, verse forty-two.

In the light of Dodd's discussion of this "return" of Christ to "finish His work" and the recognition that "the expectation of a very early advent persisted so long in the Church," it is surprising how critics of Dodd have restricted

---

[1] Dodd, *Apostolic Preaching, op. cit.,* p. 42.

his interpretation of eschatology as exclusively limited to what has already happened.[2] To this we have previously referred and further consideration is not needed. Our present task is to look at the implications of this idea of an anticipated consummation of the redemptive work of God in Christ.

There was a time when to speak of the Second Coming of Christ would brand one as some sort of Adventist. It may be a little unfortunate that the idea has again become respectable. To espouse a point of view because it is current, the fad of the moment, may be the mark of contemporaneity, but it is manifestly not the method of responsible theological thought. At any rate, since Evanston, to use a convenient date, one may speak of the Parousia without being listed as a fanatic. A well-known continental theologian, visiting with a liberal of an earlier day, referred to a third Biblical scholar. The liberal friend said: "Why, he actually believes in the Second Coming of Christ." Whereupon, the continental scholar surprised him with this reply: "Well, don't you?"

In spite of the popular parson who reacted against the theme of Evanston by decrying the pessimism of "those blessed continentals," with the plea, "Let's get on with the job!" likely we shall live within a revival of this theme for many years. Whether we begin with the Apostles' Creed and its claim that Christ will "come to judge the quick and the dead," or with the liturgy of the Church of South India:

> Thy death, O Lord, we commemorate;
> Thy resurrection we confess;
> And Thy second coming we await,[3]

or with the resurgence of theological interest in eschatology, it adds up to this certainty: the promise of the return of Christ

---

[2] *Ibid.,* pp. 64f.

[3] Newbigin, *Sin and Salvation, op. cit.,* p. 117.

cannot be legitimately excised from the New Testament. The late Professor William Manson has written a most discriminating analysis of the Eschatology of the Parousia. He argues that there is "a realized eschatology. There is also an eschatology of the unrealized." [4] And from the above reference in Acts 3:20f, Manson argues that the early Christians believed that the Son of Man would appear again on earth. The earth is to be the scene of the final redemption wrought by Christ. The Reign of God, while certain within history, "points to a further stage in the unfolding of the *Eschaton*." Thus "The Christian eschatology of glory cannot therefore, be dismissed as a lag-over or residuum from Judaism." There is a point not yet reached, not even yet in sight. Therefore,

> The Christianity of the New Testament, while it is pervaded throughout by the sense of fulfilling the law and the prophets and thus of representing the Era of Redemption, creates its own *Eschatology of Glory* centering in the Parousia of Christ.... The curve of the *Eschaton* has intersected the orbit of our historical life. One focus has taken position in the Incarnation of Christ; the other, the Second Advent, lies beyond our horizon and power to conceive.[5]

SHEER FINALITY

Previously we have referred to Dodd's claim that his "realized eschatology" contains all that is needful to understand the New Testament except the element of "sheer Finality." [6] What, now, may be subsumed under this term as we look forward toward the future?

The least we can say is that the Christian lives in expectation. Present human achievements are temporary. Even in our best schemes there is an element of disintegration. Amid our

---

[4] "Eschatology," *op. cit.*, p. 7.

[5] *Ibid.*, pp. 8, 11, 14, 15.

[6] Dodd, *op. cit.*, p. 231.

happiest successes we encounter decay. "In the midst of life we are in death" is the word of the Burial Service.

This is poignantly expressed by Robert Bridges, Poet Laureate of Britain following the Great War of 1914-18. He vividly describes the horrors which finally led to victory—but not without restless apprehensions:

> Alas then in what plight are we, knowing 'twas mankind's crowded uncleanness of soul that brought our plague! which yet we could not cure nor stay; for Reason had lost control of his hot-temper'd steed and taken himself infection of the wild brute's madness; so when its fire slacken'd and the fierce fight wore out, our fever'd pulse show'd no sober return of health.
>
> Amid the flimsy joy of the uproarious city my spirit on those first jubilant days of armistice was heavier within me, and felt a profounder fear than ever it knew in all the War's darkest dismay.[7]

A symbol of this deterioration has more recently been seen in the refusal of the Very Reverend C. C. Thicknesse, Dean of St. Albans, to permit the cathedral to be used for a Victory Thanksgiving after the dropping of the atomic bomb. V-J Day, however significant in ending the war earlier than otherwise would have been, unleashed demonic elements which may yet bring us to ruin.

Yet this is not all. Brunner is right: The early Christians participated in an event, "in something which has happened, which is happening, and which is going to happen." [8] It is this participation even now in something which is "going to happen" which the New Testament describes as a promise, a pledge, a deposit, an installment, already a guarantee of God's future recreativity. (See Ephesians 1:14; II Corinthians 1:22;

---

[7] Robert Bridges, *The Testament of Beauty* (London: Oxford University Press, 1929), p. 80.

[8] Emil Brunner, *Man in Revolt*, translated by Olive Wyon (Philadelphia: The Westminster Press, 1947), p. 494.

5:5; Romans 8:16f) "The Holy Spirit is the gift of God's presence and power within us in this life and the pledge of the fulness of the divine life that will be ours in the Age to Come." [9]

Professor Filson summarizes the importance of a Christian eschatology in three propositions: (1) It says "something essential about God." Christian faith cannot escape the conviction that God will pursue His purpose through to its perfect conclusion. "To regard this present tangled world situation as our last word about God would be fatal to New Testament faith. Eschatology is necessary to a satisfying faith in God." [10] (2) It likewise speaks of faith in human destiny. Life obviously does not deal out fair treatment nor offer fulfillment in this world to all who seek the good life. But integral to the Christian faith is some claim and call for fruition. (3) It likewise sets the world conflict in proper perspective.[11] Though evil seems victorious and goodness doomed, the power of evil carries the seeds of its own destruction. Inherent in goodness is the survival power to overcome its enemies. God will bring to a final consummation all things in a manner commensurate with His power and wisdom. Thus Filson finds a convergence among Biblical scholars claiming that the Kingdom is "new, now, but still incomplete." [12] "This is eschatology already begun, in process of being realized more fully, and certain to come to complete realization." [13]

It is this inescapable fact that we live in a dying world yet are unable to shake off the conviction that dying is not the final word which requires some word about the future—and the present.

---

[9] Richardson, *An Introduction to the Theology of the New Testament, op. cit.,* p. 116.
[10] Filson, *Jesus Christ the Risen Lord, op. cit.,* pp. 260f.
[11] *Ibid.,* p. 261.
[12] *Ibid.,* p. 102.
[13] *Ibid.,* p. 263.

A CHRISTIAN PHILOSOPHY
OF HISTORY

Georges Florovsky has vigorously reminded us that Christianity is incurably a historical religion. It makes an explicit appeal to history and bears "a witness of faith to certain particular events in the past, to certain particular data of history" as emphasis is put on "the ultimate cruciality of certain historic events, namely, of the Incarnation, of the Coming of the Messiah, and of his Cross and Resurrection." [14] Florovsky, while recognizing the current value of an existential approach to historical events, and of the necessity of some measure of demythologization, holds that such disciplines can become the enemy not only of the Christian faith but of any intelligible understanding of history itself. He claims that the emphasis upon "historicity" of much existential study is "neither historical nor distinctively Christian." It is, rather, in many instances, "a relapse into Hellenism." As he says:

> 'Man's historicity' means, in certain existentialist interpretations, nothing more than man's essential temporality, his inextricable involvement in the comprehensive context of passing occurrences, which brings him finally, to extinction, to death. This diagnosis reminds one, however, more of the tragic insight of the Ancients than of the jubilant News of the Gospel.[15]

But it must not be thought that this Christian understanding of historical data has been without its rivals. For example, there has been the persistent Greek idea of recurring cycles. If human existence on the earth be merely the repetition of

---

[14] Georges Florovsky, "The Predicament of the Christian Historian," in *Religion and Culture*, Walter Leibrecht, Editor (New York: Harper & Brothers, 1959), p. 140.

[15] *Ibid.*, p. 163.

things which once were, and which are destined sooner or later to reappear, in a monotonous inevitability, obviously any sense of human freedom or divine grace is precluded. In such a cosmic course of events, in terms of growth and decay, or of mere repetition, the significance of man, especially man under God, is absent. As Florovsky says: "There was a *rhythm* in the cosmic process, and consequently in the destiny of man, but *no direction*. History was not going or moving anywhere. It was only rotating." [16] Against this view is to be set the Christian claim that God's action is *Heilsgeschichte,* holy history or history of salvation, that is, the historical story of the redemptive, recreative deeds of the Almighty Father.

Christianity also must confront the philosophy of doom. Oswald Spengler claims that human destiny moves from infancy to growing up into adulthood, then comes senility and death—all to be repeated yet again. This has had popular appeal, not only among pessimistic souls, but it seeps now and again into the pulpit. It is not difficult to find clues in political and social turmoil to a chaos which shall include even an apocalyptic ruin. The enthusiasm of youthful preachers, when confronted by sins they cannot cure, at times tends toward this gloomy prophecy. An eminent bishop, known as a prophet of hope in the midst of the darkest despair, once admitted he had been, early in his career, a prophet of doom.

There is the view of history as calamitous. Things are bad. They are getting worse. As soon as they get sufficiently evil, God will intervene to punish all the wicked and reward all the good. It is strange that if we divide all people into two groups—the good and the bad, it is always the good people who know who belongs to which! This is the apocalyptic mood which expects God to crush our enemies—presumably our enemies are His enemies as well. Even the resurrection did not exorcize this demon from the disciples—on the eve of Pentecost, they

---

[16] *Ibid.,* p. 160.

could still ask: "Lord, is this the time when You are going to restore the Kingdom to Israel?" (Acts 1:6)

We are all tempted at times to espouse a tragic view of history. But in our best moods we know this can never be squared with the Gospel. A philosophy of ruin would leave not only man, but God, in jeopardy—since God has identified Himself with man in his predicament.

But one of the most widespread threats to a Christian philosophy of history has been the idea of progress. This is inherited from our scientific mood. Human history is seen as on a spiral staircase, perhaps an escalator, headed for the stars. This is the modern tower of Babel. It is optimistically expressed in famous lines which, believe it or not, at times is sung:

> I will not cease from Mental Fight,
> Nor shall my Sword sleep in my hand
> Till we have built Jerusalem
> In England's green & pleasant Land.[17]

Blake's dreams have vanished. In England sturdy souls may have built London and Manchester, rebuilt Coventry and Plymouth, and erected a new hope at Harwell. But Jerusalem still belongs elsewhere. And even in Jerusalem a Messiah may lose His life. Whatever else the last quarter century has taught us—we now know there is no final trust in inevitable progress. Archibald MacLeish may be a bit cynical, but he senses this denouement of history:

The conquest of the cosmos by Science. But it is no Lordship. It gives mankind no position of honor. It is no more a conquest than the collection of rain is a conquest of rain. It is finding out How. You learn what you can do with electricity. A monkey learns what it can do with a nut. The great modern sickness of boredom has its

---

17 William Blake, From "Milton," Preface, Stanza 4.

roots there. We do not wish to be kings. We wish to know How.
And we know. And we are bored. To death.[18]

To refer again to Dodd: "The Gospel does not speak of
'progress,' but of dying and rising again. The pattern of history is revealed less in evolution than in crisis." [19] This is a
far cry from our persistent plea to "bring in the Kingdom," to
"build the Kingdom," or even our song to "bring in the day
of brotherhood and end the night of wrong." [20] Christian
eschatology means that God's people are set within the context
of all history, that God takes the tangled, soiled, broken strands
of human life and weaves them into a pattern for redemption.
It means that history does not carry its own fulfilment, though
it may carry its own ruin! It means that God takes history
seriously. For history is the convergence of natural law, human
freedom, and divine grace. And human freedom lies between
natural law and divine grace as the expression of man's co-crea-
tivity (or discreativity) with God in the consummation of all
things.

"Until He comes!" The idea of the Second Coming gives
the clue to a Christian philosophy of history, a history which
is called *"heilsgeschichte"* in which "the whole of history, even
'the hopeless history of the world,' appears now *in the perspective of an ultimate, eschatological conflict."* [21]

THIS DAY—THE DAY OF
THE LORD!

Basically, what did the hope of the "day of the Lord" mean
to the disciples in the early Church? Amid all the academic

---

18 Archibald MacLeish, *A Time to Speak* (Boston: Houghton Mifflin Company, 1941), p. 157.
19 Dodd, *op. cit.,* p. 238.
20 William Pierson Merrill, in *Methodist Hymnal,* No. 267.
21 Florovsky, *op. cit.,* p. 164.

discussion of texts, contemporary literature, and Messianic analysis, doubtless each of us has tried to think himself back into the atmosphere of those days in an attempt to imagine what really constituted the hope of a return of Christ. I am not convinced such intricate and detailed speculations have thrown too much light on the matter. For my part, I am persuaded that those primitive Christians had a rather uncritical, even naive, hope that any day, today or tomorrow, might be the climax of God's divine purpose for history. This would mean not so much a datable, historical, event as a *mood of expectancy*. They greeted the sunrise of each morning with that eagerness that it might be the day when God's eternal sun would rise and never set. They were to live as if every day were their last. Every day, any day, could be the day when God would act again as decisively as He had acted at Bethlehem and at Calvary.

As early as First Thessalonians, in spite of the "misunderstanding" of Paul's letter, this hope is expressed: "Your whole lives now look forward to the coming of His Son from Heaven." (I Thessalonians 1:10) but since you "are not living in darkness the day cannot take you completely by surprise." (I Thessalonians 5:4) There is evidence that Paul believed he would live to see that glorious day. In Romans he can say: "The present time is of the highest importance—it is time to wake up to reality. Every day brings God's salvation nearer." (Romans 13:11) Even if in one of his later epistles Paul seems to feel he may not be alive at the Parousia, he can still say to the Philippian Christians: "I want you to be able always to recognize the highest and the best, and to live sincere and blameless lives until the day of Jesus Christ." (Philippians 1:10) I am not sure Phillips has preserved the deepest sense of Paul's mood in Philippians 4:5; the original Greek seems to imply more than "the nearness of your Lord." It is substantially equivalent to the famous Μαρὰν ἀθά ("Our Lord, come") of I Corinthians 16:23, and might be rendered: "The Lord is exceedingly near," or "He is coming soon."

In other New Testament passages, the parable of the absentee Landlord (Luke 12:36-40) illustrates this constant watchfulness at every hour, every day. A similar hope would be generated by the promise in Acts 3:20f: "Then He will send you Jesus, your long-heralded Christ, although for the time He must remain in Heaven until that universal Restoration of which God spoke in ancient times through all His Holy Prophets." In the Johannine writings such expressions as these could not but encourage a persistent hope for God's further intervention: "I am not going to leave you alone in the world—I am coming to you." (John 14:18) "In a little while you will not see Me any longer, and again, in a little while you will see Me." (John 16:16) "Now you are going through pain, but I shall see you again and your hearts will thrill with joy." (John 16:22) "So our love for Him grows more and more, filling us with complete confidence for the day when He shall judge all men." (I John 4:17) And three times in the Apocalypse there is a liturgical formula, "Surely I am coming soon," with the reply: "Amen. Come, Lord Jesus!" (Revelation 22:7, 12, 20, RSV) It is not too much to say that the permeating mood of the New Testament is summarized in the words of Jesus: "Be on the alert—for you do not know the day or the time." (Matthew 25:13) We cannot do better than to note the confidence expressed by the late T. W. Manson: "Whether the Final Consummation comes soon or late, suddenly or gradually, it is bound to come if the name 'Kingdom of God' corresponds to anything real: and unless the Spirit of adoption whereby we cry, 'Abba, Father' is a lying spirit, the faithful in the present age must have a share in its glory when it comes." [22]

---

[22] T. W. Manson, *The Teaching of Jesus* (London and New York: Cambridge University Press, 1948), p. 284.

This mood of expectancy is seen in the contrast between two New Testament terms for "time," *chronos* and *kairos*. I concur with John Marsh and other scholars that we must look, not to the Hellenistic culture for the New Testament significance of these words, but to the LXX which "embody the meanings with which the Hebrew words of the Old Testament are charged." [23] But *chronos* fits no Old Testament expression; it is essentially a term describing duration, successiveness, possibly even clock or almanac time. The time the star appeared (Matthew 2:7), the long time the impotent man had been at the pool (John 5:6), the sorcerer had intimidated the people for a long time (Acts 8:11), the wife is bound to her husband as long as he lives (I Corinthians 7:39), the writer of the Hebrews does not have sufficient time to recount the histories of all the heroes of the faith. (Hebrews 11:32)

As for *kairos*, it refers to a suitable time, an appropriate opportunity, a special occasion. The "signs of the times" have in them a qualitative significance. (Matthew 16:3) For Mark "the time is fulfilled" by the coming of Christ. (Mark 1:15) The special times of God's actions are unknown by the wisdom of men since He holds them under his own authority. (Acts 1:7) It was at the time when "we were powerless to help ourselves that Christ died for sinful men." (Romans 5:6) Early religious ceremonies were valid only until "the time when Christ should establish the truth." (Hebrews 9:10) Thus Tillich can conclude that *chronos* points to a measurable side of time, "the quantitative, calculable, repetitive element of the temporal process; while *kairos* emphasizes the qualitative, experiential, unique element." [24]

"Until He Comes" then means that each moment of "time" is charged with eternal significance, that we live in this qualita-

---

23 Marsh, *The Fulness of Time, op. cit.*, p. 76.

24 Paul Tillich, *Handbook of Christian Theology,* Living Age Books (New York: Meridian Books, Inc., 1958), p. 194.

tive dimension of time which is alive with the meaning of God's redemptive presence.

Thus to live in This Day as the Day of the Lord is to live in the midst of revolution—God's recreative love penetrating by transforming each day with divine significance. A French attorney has stressed this revolutionary nature of the kingdom here and now. Jacques Ellul says: "It is the imminence of the Return of Christ which gives genuine seriousness to each actual event," for example, each event in time as *chronos* becomes an event in time as *kairos* when it becomes the vehicle of Christian faith in the imminent Return of Christ.[25] Thus "Every Christian who has received the Holy Spirit is now a prophet of the Return of Christ, and by this very fact he has a revolutionary mission in politics." [26]

The early Christians lived under the conviction that the time was short. The last days had already come. They were living under an intense urgency. Their creed was simple: "Jesus is Lord." (See Romans 10:9; I Corinthians 12:3; Philippians 2:11) But it was a creed of men alive with the presence of their Living Lord. E. Stanley Jones tells how this central Christian affirmation has swept through the Christian Ashrams under the symbol of the upraised hand with three fingers. He is Lord, Lord of many things, and certainly Lord of the future. The believer is not slavishly attached to the past. He is living at the growing edge of tomorrow's certainty—under God. The great days of the faith are never mere memories—however glorious. A dear friend once a bit pessimistically asked me when we were going back to the "good old days." I replied: "Thank God, we never are!" The only days we have are *from now on.* The conviction that This Day is the Day of the Lord gives to each day the dimension of the Parousia.

The Return of Christ, then, is the affirmation of the final

---

[25] Jacques Ellul, *The Presence of the Kingdom,* Translated by Olive Wyon (Philadelphia: The Westminster Press, 1952), p. 50.

[26] *Ibid.,* p. 50.

triumph of righteousness, since the victory has already been won in His first coming. The Holy Spirit, who bears to us the benefits of Christ's victory, is a "taste," or "first-fruits," a "down payment," of this ultimate victory and thus guarantees the future in the experience of the present. "You were, so to speak, stamped with the promised Holy Spirit as a guarantee of purchase, until the day when God completes the redemption of what He has paid for as his own; and that will again be to the praise of His glory." (Ephesians 1:14)

I must here raise a protest against ill-advised tamperers with the liturgy of Holy Communion. It is no mark of theological wisdom to delete the words "until his coming again" from the prayer of consecration. Granted that we may not want to be as literal as some adventists would suggest, but this does not mean we can ignore that the Holy Eucharist is a foretaste of the Messianic banquet and marriage supper of the Lamb. The Church is the eschatological community. As it meets in its sacramental fellowship, it is not a mere memory of an event long in the past. It is not only a participation in the present *koinonia*. It is a foreshadowing of that blessed day when the Risen Lord shall be with His people in the ultimate kingdom. This liturgy is a memorial of His death. But it is also a symbol of His sacrifice for the sins of the whole world. And it is the certainty of His Presence at each table, "Until He Comes!"

WILL ALL BE SAVED?

To refer to the eschatological hope is to raise the question not only of the redeemed—but of the question as to whether or no all shall finally submit to God's love and mercy. Whatever be our view, this question is up for discussion. And whether we approve or no, the claim that some might be forever banished from the presence of God is distasteful to many.

It would seem that there are two ways to interpret a possible salvation for all people. There is, first, the view that a benevolent Deity could not endure the loss of a single soul. This position tends to minimize the seriousness of sin. God is the father of all men. All men are brothers. What we call sin is only a stage in the divine education of immature children. No rejection is sufficiently serious to separate any person from blessedness forever. This view, I hasten to add, has few advocates today—though it has had some approval in the past.

The other view is rooted in God understood in terms of *agape,* that is, unselfish, outgoing, creative love. Divine love is seen as being so powerfully operative that it will finally overcome the neglect and rebellion of the lost soul—every soul outside the present kingdom. Somewhere, sometime, somehow —*agape* will pursue the last impenitent soul with such compassion that it will finally submit. Only as hell is completely emptied can heaven be heaven. This, if I understand him, is substantially the view of Nels F. S. Ferré.

There are some who cannot be quite so optimistic, since their view of human freedom includes the possibility of a final and persistent rejection. Yet also for them the idea of eternal punishment is unacceptable. Thus there has arisen the idea sometimes called "conditional immortality." Eternal life has conditions. Those who meet the conditions provided for in the gracious action of a Redeeming God, will possess the blessedness of the saints. Those who fail to meet the conditions will perish as if they had never been.

What can be said? Is there a place for some timid suggestions on this controverted subject?

The humane instinct which prompts us to hope that all men may be saved is in itself a sound and creditable feeling. Certainly the task of the witness for Christ is not to increase the population of hell. The Gospel is Glad Tidings designed to keep people out of it, and to get it out of people.

Yet there are some questions which persist: One of these

pertains to human freedom. If we take freedom seriously, we must at least theoretically admit the possibility to make a final choice against the right. Moral living means the possibility of moral wrongdoing. And unless we advocate the view that human freedom is a temporary phenomenon, there remains a a possibility the final rejection of the love even of the Sovereign God.

Again, all we know about human personality points in the direction of a growing fixedness, toward a more certain permanence. The longer we persist in a direction, the less likelihood there is of radical change. The longer we live the more we become what we have chosen to be. Is there any less likelihood that this tendency will be reversed in the next life?

We may certainly believe that the God of universal love wills the salvation of all men, and that the finally lost are lost entirely through their own action in defiance of His will. The final rejection, persistence in rebellion, against divine love is not a divine failure. It may even be regarded as a divine victory: to sustain the free soul in its full range of possibilities—until divine love has literally exhausted itself both in personal suffering in Calvary and subsequently in its persuasive resources —and still the recalcitrant soul says "No!"

I have come to be sympathetic with a view which asserts that all may not eventually submit to love's entreaty. Yet the day will finally come when Christ shall be Lord of all of the lost— as well as of the blessed. There will be those who "bow the knee" joyfully and who persist in a fellowship begun in this life, and in many respects not essentially different from the noblest heights of Christian joy known on earth. For those who refuse—there will be the existence involved in their eternal necessity, created by their own sins. It may be characterized as the loss of freedom, hence of the loss of the power of rebellion. They exist under necessity, the necessity of their own creation. Every soul must choose what his service of God will be—either in freedom of love or bondage of lostness.

C. S. Lewis writes of the future in a book which might be described as a bus trip to hell: "All that are in Hell, choose it. Without that self-choice there could be no Hell. No soul that seriously and constantly desires joy will ever miss it. Those who seek find. To those who knock it is opened." [27] And in the same study he cries out against the blasphemy that hell should be able finally to blaspheme heaven. "I know it has a grand sound to say ye'll accept no salvation which leaves even one creature in the dark outside. But watch that sophistry or ye'll make a Dog in a Manger the tyrant of the universe." [28] He then pictures Hell so small that it will fit entirely into some little crack, "smaller than one pebble of your earthly world."

> For a damned soul is nearly nothing: it is shrunk, shut up in itself. Good beats upon the damned incessantly as sound waves beat on the ears of the deaf, but they cannot receive it. Their fists are clenched, their teeth are clenched, their eyes fast shut. First they will not, in the end they cannot, open their hands for gifts, or their mouths for food, or their eyes to see.[29]

How well John Whale says it:

> Christian doctrine has always urged that life eternal is something which may conceivably be missed. . . . It is illogical to tell men that they must do the will of God and accept his gospel of grace, if you also tell them that the obligation has no eternal significance, and that nothing ultimately depends on it. The curious modern heresy that everything is bound to come right in the end is so frivolous that I will not insult you by refuting it.[30]

---

27 Lewis, *The Great Divorce, op. cit.,* p. 69.
28 *Ibid.,* p. 124.
29 *Ibid.,* pp. 126f.
30 Whale, *op. cit.,* p. 186.

WHAT OF THE FUTURE?

There is a strange fascination about the mystery of the beyond. We have lived through the era when critics would speak with scorn of the otherworldliness of the Christian faith. One world is not enough for men made in the divine image. Only he whose vision is not circumscribed by the limitations of the historical scene can see the significance of the historical. This world is seen in its true perspective only in the light of that life which is eternal. As Whale so well says: "Christian doctrine is unmistakably explicit about 'the life of the Age to Come,' for which the Church of God on earth is preparation, forehint and foretaste." [31]

WHAT THEN OF THE FUTURE?

For one thing, we may assume the future is not essentially different from the present. There will not only be more of it—it will be qualitatively more glorious, with all the limitations, evils and frustrations of the present eliminated. The Church has followed a true tradition in believing that the way one lives here and now will be the way one lives there and then. Dante spoke more than poetically when he portrayed the adulterers forever pursuing each other—without satisfaction. The gossipers would forever engage in meaningless chatter. And anger would arise like bubbles bursting on the surface of calm water—from the boiling heat of inner life of those who "burn up" with hostility. And in blessedness there is likewise an extension of blessedness begun here.

Again, the major emphasis is upon fellowship, the community of those committed to God. It is conceivable that heaven will provide the mutual completion of personality through the

---

[31] *Ibid.*, p. 184.

redeemed lives of others who also need other redeemed souls to complete their existence. If the Hebrew writer could say of the heroes of the faith that "it was not His Plan that they should reach perfection without us" (Hebrews 11:40), we may likewise assume that we shall not be complete without them.

Again, we may assume the future will be the opportunity to learn and practice the full will of God. In the view of the present writer, a static heaven with all problems solved, all tasks finished, all achievements complete, would not be heaven at all; it would be, hell!

The meaningfulness of the future depends upon the final Lordship of Christ. The simple faith of Paul's early letter is still valid: after whatever strange and unknown events may characterize the Parousia, he could still say: "And after that we shall be with Him for ever." (I Thessalonians 4:17)

This much is certain: we live in a world subject to decay, a mortal world. Written deep in the structure of the creativity of God is inevitable disintegration. Only in the light of divine re-creativity, seen in the redemptive deed of Christ and the continued ministry of the Holy Spirit, is there a clear affirmation of Christian eschatology. Whale is right: "Christian eschatology means that the true evaluation of this world must rest against the background of its impermanence." [32] Phillips has caught this mood in his paraphrase of the exhortation of First Timothy:

> Keep your commission clean and above reproach until the final coming of Christ. This will be, in His own time, the Final Denouement of God, Who is the blessed controller of all things, the King over all kings and the Master of all masters, the only Source of Immortality, the One Who lives in unapproachable Light, the One Whom no mortal eye has ever seen or ever can see. To Him be acknowledged all honour and power for ever, Amen!
>
> *I Timothy, 6:14f*

---

[32] *Ibid.*, p. 184.

SEVEN

The Gospel Of New Life

An Episcopal clergyman, concerned to interpret "the release of spiritual power" available for churchmen, says:

Thousands of people in the churches as well as outside them need to hear the peremptory word of Christ, 'Ye must be born again.' Something so drastic and radical, so transforming and upheaving, must come to us ordinary folk that it is like beginning life all over again, being born again from above.[1]

Evangelists are now being joined by psychiatrists, social workers, medical doctors, scientists, businessmen, and educators, in urging that life, to be lived at its best, needs renewal

---

[1] Samuel M. Shoemaker, *By the Power of God* (New York: Harper & Brothers, 1954), p. 28.

from beyond human resources. Terminology may differ, but the growing consensus is that man is unable to reconstruct his own broken moral life by himself.

Unless kerygmatic theology issues in some clear witness to "a power not ourselves which makes for righteousness" it will remain a mere academic discipline. But the final emphasis of the kerygma, in Dodd's interpretation, confronts us with an offer: "The *kerygma* always closes with an appeal for repentance, the offer of forgiveness and of the Holy Spirit, and the promise of 'salvation,' that is, of 'the life of the Age to Come,' to those who enter the elect community." [2] The New Testament language is: "You must repent and every one of you must be baptized in the Name of Jesus Christ, so that you may have your sins forgiven and receive the gift of the Holy Spirit." (Acts 2:38) (See also Acts 3:19, 25f; 4:12; 5:31; 10:43.)

Thus there is point to Shoemaker's thrust: "Some of us have not got so far as to be converted: we have only been a little civilized by our religion." [3] If there is any truth in Kierkegaard's historic remark that it is the "good man farthest from God," it may be it is the "civilized" man who is most difficult to move to conversion. What if the kerygma were really to come to full blaze with the evangel it seeks to define? It could be the agent for the drastic and radical transformation needed not only for the emotions of men but for their minds as well.

THE NEED FOR NEW LIFE

F. R. Barry has reminded us that there is no use in exhorting men to be religious while the whole framework of their lives is directed to profoundly irreligious purposes. Then he says: "A radical redirection is necessary—that is, in religious vo-

---

[2] Dodd, *Apostolic Preaching and Its Developments, op. cit.*, p. 43.
[3] Shoemaker, *op. cit.*, p. 104.

cabulary, Conversion." [4] Or, the judgment of D. T. Niles may be cited: "The Christian message cannot be grafted upon other beliefs or added to them. There is only one way in which the Christian message can be accepted and that is by a radical conversion to it, so radical that the New Testament speaks of it as a new birth (John 3:3; I Pet. 1:3), the coming into being of a new creation (II Cor. 5:17), a dying and a living again (Rom. 6:5-8)." [5]

Finally, at this point the insight of Paul Tillich may summarize the need for new Life: "The New Being is not something that simply takes the place of the Old Being. But it is a renewal of the Old which has been corrupted, distorted, split and almost destroyed. But not wholly destroyed. Salvation does not destroy creation; but it transforms the Old Creation into a New One. Therefore we can speak of the New in terms of a *re*-newal: The threefold "re," namely, *re*-conciliation, *re*-union, *re*-surrection." [6]

But the need for new life is rooted even more deeply than in the opinions of churchmen; it is indelible in human experience. There is the frustrating fact that I am unable to rebuild the brokenness of my own moral conflicts. I encounter the fact that the most depraved man in the community has a higher knowledge of what is right than the best man puts into practice. The more saintly a person becomes the more he is persuaded that whatever righteousness he may possess is due, not to his own resources, but to the grace of God. It is most disconcerting that it is not my worst efforts to be good, but my most successful ones which reveal to me my moral weakness. As Paul could say: "I have the will to do good, but not the power." (Romans 7:18)

---

[4] F. R. Barry, *Recovery of Man* (New York: Charles Scribner's Sons, 1949), p. 45.

[5] D. T. Niles, *The Preacher's Task and the Stone of Stumbling* (New York: Harper & Brothers, 1958), p. 99.

[6] Paul Tillich, *The New Being* (New York: Charles Scribner's Sons, 1955), pp. 19f.

In the ethical struggle there is always the drift toward the wrong, whereas a conscious effort, a discipline, even an agony (Luke 13:24) is required to move into the right. John Whale has quoted a classic thought from the Gifford Lectures of Edwyn Bevan: "When people say that man is naturally good or that his good and bad impulses are pretty evenly matched, how is it that all over the world to follow the good impulses has seemed like going uphill, and to follow the evil ones like going downhill?" [7]

Sometimes the need for new life is seen in the doubleness, the dividedness, the duality in personal living. "The life of a man of divided loyalty will reveal instability at every turn" is the witness of James. (James 1:8) A student, seeking to express this duality, spoke of the "D-U-E-L" nature of man! A failure in spelling, perfect score in theology!

Sometimes the need is focused against the background of self-centeredness. It has been suggested that ego-centricity is a good term for this condition of human nature. Or, it may be seen as the glory of self, the subtle sin of pride. No one is in more danger of the sin of pride than he who is persuaded of his humility. John Baillie speaks of the "regressive character of human sinfulness." By this he means that we become aware of our pride and then repent. This makes us become aware of our repentance and hence proud of our awareness, and so on. [8] I once wrote to a world-famous theologian asking if he would suggest a dozen definitive theological monographs of the twentieth century. He obliged, after saying he didn't really have time to reply to such requests, by listing two of his own publications! Technically, I think he was correct. But it would have been more convincing had he permitted someone else to cite his masterpieces—or, at least, to have limited his selection to one.

Even the metaphor of death may be used. The New Testa-

---

[7] Whale, *Christian Doctrine, op. cit.,* p. 49.
[8] Baillie, *Invitation to Pilgrimage, op. cit.,* p. 59.

ment speaks of the deadness of the natural man. In a discussion group concerned with the sickness of modern man, I asked a quiet student from Holland to comment. He replied significantly: "In Holland we do not say, 'Man is sick'; in Holland we say, "Man is dead.' " Then he added the clarifying thought: "Dead in trespasses and sins."

I have the uncomfortable feeling that our recent proclivity toward liturgical religion, the drift into forms and ceremonies, can be an evidence of the need for new life. How slowly do we learn that it is much easier to light another candle than to have the soul illuminated by the Holy Spirit. It is more convenient to chant another response than to sing a song of deliverance from sin. A litany requires less commitment than the experience of intercession in a prayer cell. And one may frequent the Holy Eucharist with monkish regularity and never have one's soul lifted in true thanksgiving to God for the inner certainty of the Holy Spirit. Nor is this view confined to those who find more profit in "free" worship. Shoemaker, writing from *within* the liturgical tradition, indicates "that other things being equal it is easier to put on the harness of the sacramental system, to make it the be-all-and-end-all, and idolize it, than it is to work and strive to turn one's inner life over to God so deeply that spiritual power may come in and through one's life." [9]

Unless I am totally mistaken, there is now a hunger for a religious life which offers more than the mere proper performance of ceremonies—however beautiful and correct. We have been thrust into conditions which demonstrate the need for new life. We may control our worst selves by sitting upon the explosive quality of vicious conduct. But we know that the inner struggle is not curbed by discipline. Even preaching on, or against, the current crop of popular iniquities can do more harm than good. If our ministries leave the impression that by

---

[9] Shoemaker, *op. cit.,* pp. 124f.

avoiding the dramatic forms of wickedness we are thereby righteous, it may encourage complacent trust in a false assurance, the inner self remaining corrupt. The worst sins in our land never happen. They simply fester and poison the inner springs of life. Dorothy Sayers asks the question: "What does the church call sin?" Then she answers: "Sex . . . ; getting drunk, saying 'damn'; murder, and cruelty to dumb animals; not going to church; most kinds of amusement. 'Original sin' means that anything we enjoy doing is wrong." [10] Her irony has a sting in it. The sins which bedevil our land are not basically the well-advertised variety. Generally speaking, even the professionally wicked man feels they shouldn't be practiced. But the sins which eat the heart out of us are: resentment, ill will, prejudice, oppression of minority groups, ambition, prideful self-seeking, critical attitudes, and the like.

The lack of new life could confirm us in spiritual death. We are driven to see that nothing short of radical remaking of character by the power of God is sufficient. The trouble is not in our ignorance, our confusion, our environment, our stupidity, our heritage (though, God knows, these are sufficiently perverted). We are sick at heart. We must be reborn to be healed.

WHAT THE GOSPEL OFFERS

The apostolic preaching, the kerygma, was a call to repentance in order to new life. The New Testament language is quite clear: "You must not be surprised that I told you that all of you must be born again." (John 3:7) This is both an offer and a demand.

What is offered is not merely a covering up of the defects of the old life. It is change into an entirely new sort of living. It is the difference suggested by the contrast between life and

---

[10] Dorothy Sayers, *Creed or Chaos?* (New York: Harcourt, Brace & World, Inc., © Dorothy L. Sayers, 1949), pp. 22f.

death. Those who hear and believe the Gospel have "already passed from death into life." (John 5:24) God's "peculiar people" are "to demonstrate the goodness of Him Who has called you out of darkness into His amazing Light." (I Peter 2:9) Those who have been buried with Christ are raised "to life on a new plane altogether." (Romans 6:4) But no one has said it more adequately than Paul in his words to the church at Corinth: "For if a man is in Christ he becomes a new person altogether—the past is finished and gone, everything has become fresh and new." (II Corinthians 5:17)

It seems obvious that such a radical change cannot be expressed by a single term. Thus both Scripturally and theologically there is a variety of expressions used to describe the offer of the Gospel. For example, there is the word *redemption*. The idea here is that of the emancipation of the slave. The experience of deliverance was well-known in Hebrew history, whether from Egypt or from Babylon. But in the New Testament it reaches an even more lofty conception of freedom from the bondage of sin. "Christ has redeemed us from the curse of the Law's condemnation." (Galatians 3:13) There is a new power in Christ which lifts us "out of the old vicious circle of sin and death." (Romans 8:2) Whatever other human needs there may be, the greatest need is to be saved from sin, both personal and corporate. Hence "we must never forget that He rescued us from the power of darkness, and reestablished us in the Kingdom of His beloved Son, that is, in the Kingdom of Light. For it is by His Son alone that we have been redeemed and have had our sins forgiven." (Colossians 1:13f)

The term *conversion* at times is used. This is a psychological term, and one favored in evangelical circles. E. Stanley Jones, in a very disturbing manner, puts his finger on the central issue in conversion: "The pressure for conversion comes from the hell of having to live with a self you don't like and can't respect, a self which you hate, but with which you must daily and hourly live." Then he asks: "Can that very self be converted?" [11] It is the offer of the Gospel that it can. It is more than the change in the position of the sinner from being an unacceptable one to being an accepted one. Something deep and profound must happen at the center of one's personal life.

The late William Temple may in no sense be classified among religious extremists. Thus, when he speaks on the subject of conversion we may assume it is from a deep conviction of its central importance—especially since he discusses it in his Gifford Lectures. He argues that there must be "the sharp break which has been called, in the language of religion, conversion or the new birth; or else there may be a series of conversions affecting different areas of life; but there is need for real discontinuity." [12] And when he discusses the meaning of conversion the apostolic urgency is felt. It is important to quote at length:

> Such radical conversion must be the act of God, and that too by some process other than the gradual self-purification of a self-centered soul assisted by the ever-present influence of God diffused through nature including human nature. It cannot be a process only of enlightenment. Nothing can suffice but a redemptive act.[13]

Another term is *justification*. This is a forensic term. It comes from the Roman law courts. The old judgments are cleared away. Pardon is declared. As Paul says, "no condemnation now hangs over the head of those who are 'in' Jesus Christ." (Romans 8:1) Justification, to be meaningful at all, must include more than a pronounced absolution. If in any sense a man is to stand before God "justified," it must be not only because God deigns to look upon him with merciful favor, but also because some initial or at least potential transforma-

---

11 E. Stanley Jones, *Conversion* (Nashville: Abingdon Press, 1959), p. 50.

12 William Temple, *Nature, Man and God* (London: Macmillan and Co., Ltd., St. Martin's Press, Inc., 1935), p. 388.

13 *Ibid.*, p. 397.

tion is seen by God within him, corresponding to his changed attitude to God. We must concur with the conclusion of Vincent Taylor when he says: "If through faith a man is accounted righteous, it must be because, in a reputable sense of the term, he is righteous, and not because another is righteous in his stead." [14] C. H. Dodd would seem to support Taylor's interpretation. Speaking of the justified man, he says:

> Outwardly, he is the same man he was, open still to his neighbours' harsh judgment, liable still to condemnation under a law which balances achievement against shortcoming. But really the man is changed through and through by that act of self-committal, self-abandonment to God. Before God he is indeed dead to sin and alive in a quite new way to righteousness. In fact, he is righteous, in a fresh sense of the word. . . . A man who is in that relation to God is right. He is justified, in no fictitious way, but by the verdict of reality.[15]

And although Richardson seems to us to make the sacrament of baptism too determinative in his interpretation of justification, nevertheless his words are conclusive: "God treats us as righteous, because we are righteous in so far as we are 'in Christ.' It is not that God treats us 'as if' we were righteous. In Christ we *are* righteous even now." [16] Thus Phillips' paraphrase is to be understood in its fullest dynamic sense: "For the new spiritual principle of life 'in' Christ lifts me out of the old vicious circle of sin and death." (Romans 8:2)

The term *reconciliation* reaches beyond the slave market and the court of law to express the idea of harmony in personal relations. "God was in Christ personally reconciling the world to Himself—not counting their sins against them—and

---

[14] Vincent Taylor, *Forgiveness and Reconciliation* (London: Macmillan and Co., Ltd., St. Martin's Press, Inc., 1946), p. 57.

[15] C. H. Dodd, *The Meaning of Paul for Today* (London: George Allen Univ., Ltd., nd), pp. 110f.

[16] Richardson, *An Introduction to the Theology of the New Testament, op. cit.*, p. 237.

has commissioned us with the message of reconciliation." (II Corinthians 5:19) The one fatal factor which destroys human fellowship, with God or within the community, is sin. We have previously spoken of the power of sin as discreative, as producing a sense of isolation, the corroding experience of being an alien. Paul powerfully expresses this condition and its correction: "You yourselves, who were strangers to God, and, in fact, through the evil things you had done, His spiritual enemies, He has now reconciled through the death of His Body on the Cross, so that He might welcome you to His presence clean and pure, without blame or reproach." (Colossians 1:21f)

Closely related to this idea of reconciliation is the experience described by the term *adoption*. This metaphor suggests the context of the home. "You have been adopted into the very family circle of God and you can say with a full heart, 'Father, my Father.' " (Romans 8:15) The alien-nature of life, the unwantedness, the sense of being orphaned, the "estrangement"—to use existential speech—is banished when we are accepted into the household of God. This is more than a superficial psychological acceptance—often on the level of our own sinfulness which we accept as the best we can hope for in this life. Rather is it such an acceptance by God of our own unacceptability that His recreative power actually welcomes us into His fellowship. And this welcome begins the process of restoration into the full status of sonship.

Sometimes the word is *regeneration*. This may be considered simply in the doctrinal framework of the *ordo salutis,* the order of salvation. But it is much more meaningful than merely a theological term. It is best viewed in the context of a personal encounter with the Risen Christ. "Once the Spirit of Him who raised Jesus from the dead lives within you He will, by that same Spirit, bring to your whole being new strength and vitality." (Romans 8:11) E. Stanley Jones speaks of this new life as "God where it counts—within us." Alan Richardson says: "The sense of having been re-made in Christ pervades the NT writings." [17] But it is when we go beyond the idea, the language, the theology of regeneration, into the experience of a conferred life—nothing less than the impartation of the very life of God—that this offer of the Gospel makes sense.

Quite possibly the word *forgiveness* has taken on a new significance due to its therapeutic value—but the experience is no recent discovery. One can understand why the psychologist said he sent his patients to such and such a church since there the forgiveness of sins was earnestly proclaimed. It was Leslie Weatherhead who said: "The forgiveness of God, in my opinion, is the most powerful therapeutic idea in the world." [18] To claim that there is available a personal resource which can and does break the chain reaction of evil in one's life is a bold, daring claim. But to settle for less is not only to pervert the Gospel of forgiveness but to remain the victim of the hopeless impasse in terms of *simul justus et peccator*. The truth underlying this Reformation paradox cannot be denied. But the tendency today seems to accept the *peccator* pole. Some wit has accused the current crop of pessimistic theologians of inverting the Scriptures to say: "Where grace abounded, sin did much more abound!" If forgiveness means anything at all, it carries with it a deliverance not only from the penalty of sin but release from its power. And while it is not total emancipation (nor escape) from total sinfulness—at least it provides the certainty of a "new being" in Christ, to use Tillich's term. Those who have experienced the creative power of forgiveness can still sing with the Wesleys:

> Long my imprison'd spirit lay
> Fast bound in sin and nature's night;
> Thine eyes diffused a quick'ning ray—
> I woke; the dungeon flamed with light!

[17] *Ibid.*, p. 35.
[18] Leslie Weatherhead, *Psychology, Religion and Healing* (Nashville: Abingdon Press, 1951), p. 334.

My chains fell off, my heart was free,
I rose, went forth, and followed Thee.[19]

Thus one who has known the deep recreative powers of divine forgiveness can never accept *simul justus et peccator* as the norm for man's best.

Whatever language is used, we have a right to expect the new life of God to push deep into our lives where our own moral failures beat us down. It may well be that we shall never be saved so completely as momentarily never to step aside, but we have a right to believe we can be saved so fully that when we do wrong we do not approve it nor enjoy it. The Philippian jailer, the woman at the well, the Legion among the tombs, the quiet devotion of Nicodemus—all reveal a quality of life they did not create. It was given to them. They came to know what the Gospel offers.

WHAT THE NEW BIRTH DOES NOT DO

John Wesley is often cited as the example of the converting power of the Gospel. We make much of May 24th, 1738—as the Aldersgate experience of the "heart strangely warmed." But do we read his journal of October, 1738? Wesley detects inner desires which are quite unholy. He confesses he does not find within himself the love of God. He experiences a deadness and wandering of mind in prayer. Even his attitude toward the Holy Communion is one of cold inattention. "I have not that joy in the Holy Ghost; no settled, lasting joy. Nor have I such a peace as excludes the possibility either of fear or doubt." [20]

---

[19] *A Collection of Hymns for Public, Social, and Domestic Worship*, A. H. Redford, Nashville (1866), No. 459.

[20] John Wesley, *The Journal of the Rev. John Wesley*, Standard Edition, Edited by Nehemiah Curnock, vol. ii (London: The Epworth Press, 1938), p. 91.

Wherein is there a tendency to claim too much for the new life? For one thing, it offers no certain guarantee of admissions into heaven. Wesley knew, along with Bunyan: "Then I saw that there was a way to hell, even from the gates of heaven." [21]

Likewise, too easily we assume that the new life solves all spiritual problems. In a real sense becoming a Christian creates more problems than it solves. There is the added responsibility of putting the Gospel of new life into all human relationships. Paul's problems did not *end* on the Damascus Road; they merely *began* there. Indeed, so acute were these problems that the Apostle to the Gentiles saw the possibility that he could, even after ministering faithfully in God's Name, still make shipwreck of his faith. The possibility of utter ruin, after having made a notable beginning, hangs over the head of every saint. Moral catastrophes among those in high spiritual places too often demonstrate a dangerous dimension in human life.

Nor does a vital relationship with Christ mean we can ignore the need for daily renewal. The nurture of the Christian life bears witness both to the precarious manner in which life is lived and also to the offer of adequate divine resources for its living. The "means of grace" universally recognized within Christendom provide the discipline for sustained spiritual growth. And while the "hour of decision" has a proper place in the kerygmatic gospel, in a sense every hour is that decision hour. As important as personal surrender may be, what is really important is the state of one's present relationship to Christ.

But perhaps the most serious confusion in modern Christianity is the assumption that commitment to Christ will automatically produce social righteousness. The tragic fact confronts us: often among those persons giving most vocal attention to the need for conversion is found relatively little concern for the cure of deep-seated social maladjustments. The dramatic

---

[21] John Bunyan, *The Pilgrim's Progress,* part i, chapter xx.

example now is racial discrimination. It is a blot upon the face of modern church life that otherwise intelligent persons do rise up to defend legalized segregation by appeals to the Bible —or even to the teachings of Our Lord. To be Biblical for a moment, a careful look at the life of Simon Peter shows he was converted in installments. One came when he forsook his nets to follow Jesus. Another came after his blundering failure in the judgment hall—strangely foreshadowed in his previous demand that Jesus turn aside from the Cross! Even after the resurrection he had to be converted from the pull of the old way of life: "I'm going fishing!" (John 21:3) But no greater conversion was needed than that which delivered him from his intrenched racial prejudices against the non-Jews. In his encounter with Cornelius, Simon Peter learned that God was not pleased with his bigoted narrowness.

Unfortunately conversion does not cast out our cultural patterns rooted in the inherited idolatry of white supremacy— whether in South Africa or Southern Alabama. But we are now confronted with the fact that the white man is not going to control the world of tomorrow. No man can ally himself with the forces assigning any group in America to second-class citizenship in our society. What is needed is a radical mourner's-bench of the mind where we learn that the "Southern way of life" is not God's will for human society and that the "Christian way of life" sees beyond the color of one's skin a brotherhood of man under God. To put it quite bluntly: *Apartheid* is a Godless travesty even when promoted by a church either in Africa or in America.

TO LIVE OR NOT TO LIVE!

A recent speaker said: "If I should *die* before I *live*—." The question of living forever sems to be pushing itself into religious discussions with a new insistence. Most of us would do anything to live forever. But are we so sure we want to be alive today? It is curious how concerned we are about survival after death but how often we lack the earnestness to possess a quality of life worth perpetuating. It may well be, when we are most anxious to live forever, the kind of life we now have isn't worth it.

If I may again refer to Mr. Wesley, there seems to be a strange element in his well-known *Aldersgate* experience. For one thing, he had been searching for over ten years for a satisfying religious life; as he suggests, "fighting continually, but not conquering." And as his spiritual birthday drew near, he records a "strange indifference, dullness, and coldness, and unusually frequent relapses into sin." That afternoon of May 24, 1738, he did not go with eagerness to St. Paul to hear the choir sing: "Out of the deep have I called unto Thee." He had to be asked, to be invited, to go. Then, coming to the hour of the prayer service he says: "In the evening I went *very unwillingly—*." Most of us know this paralyzing mood when our feet drag and only with extreme effort, even against our will, we arise and go to meet God.[22]

"To live or not to live"—that is the question. There is a decisiveness in the Gospel—a sense of the urgency of this matter of life and death. It is not done with the fingers crossed. It is not casual nor optional. I once read a portion of a sermon on repentance:

> Unless you repent—it has been said,
> And confess your sins—as it were,
> Turn from your wicked ways—to an extent,
> And be converted—in a measure,
> You will be lost—so to speak!

With that message even the Church at Pentecost would have converted few people. Am I right in thinking we have silenced,

---

[22] Wesley, *op. cit.*, vol. i, pp. 470-475.

or at least quieted, this call for repentance unto life in our era of a cheap "peace of mind"—when what we need is the "peace of God which passeth all understanding"? If Paul could say: "I die daily"—can we hope to find the excellence of the Christian way if we never die at all—to those moods of complacency, unconcern, official sinfulness, and the simple unwillingness to be alive in Christ and for Christ?

This means I must surrender any personal claim I may have to the excellent way. It comes as the direct gift of God—or it doesn't come. But the issue remains: "To Live or Not to Live." This is the disjunction of the Gospel—offered by the very life of God to men.

Occasionally I ask students what would happen if, at 10:45 A.M. on Sunday—or even 11:15—they suddenly discovered some unrepentant demon had stolen their sermon notes. What does one say, in the pulpit of God—with the outline of the week's sermonic preparation gone? Then I have suggested it may be in that crisis hour the minister would learn whether or not he will preach the Gospel. For after all, the Gospel is the witness from the inmost soul of the servant of God who has wrestled "until the break of day" refusing to let God go. If in that hour the man of God bears witness to the Gospel of New Life— because he, too, is alive—he is God's prophet indeed!

EIGHT

Theology As Meeting

C. H. Dodd says: "The preaching of the Church is directed towards reconstituting in the experience of individuals the hour of decision which Jesus brought." [1] Our study of the theology of the kerygma has sought to consider some of the implications of that preaching. We must now ask what is actually involved in preaching when it comes to focus upon what may be called "theology as meeting." Or it may be expressed in other words by Dodd: "In both Testaments, then, everything turns upon an encounter of man with God." [2]

Miss Dorothy Sayers, playwright, has raised some disturbing questions in the British religious world. She classifies

---

[1] Dodd, *The Parables of the Kingdom, op. cit.*, p. 204.
[2] Dodd, *The Bible Today* (London and New York: Cambridge University Press, 1948), p. 104.

people of her country into three groups. First are the frank and open heathen, whose notions of Christianity include scraps of Bible anecdotes and clotted mythological nonsense. Then there are the ignorant Christians who combine a pink-cheeked gentle-Jesus sentimentality with vague humanistic ethics. Finally, there are the more or less instructed churchgoers who know all the proper answers to religious questions but who are utterly ineffective when met by intelligent unbelievers. In fact, Miss Sayers feels that not one person in a hundred in Great Britain has the faintest notion what the Church teaches about God, or man, or society, or the person of Jesus Christ. She then says: "Theologically, this country is at present in a state of utter chaos, established in the name of religious toleration, and rapidly degenerating into the flight from reason and the death of hope." [3]

I am not sure that Miss Sayers should be invited to America. If she finds this condition in her land, what might she find in ours? I recall it has been said that theology is *constructed* in Germany, *corrected* in Scotland, and *corrupted* in America. What hope, therefore, has the theologian/preacher today, whose task has been described as "obscuring the obvious," to recast theology in terms of interpreting the meeting of man and God? At least, what is involved in this interpretation?

For one thing, we must face the question: "How do we know?" Whether as scientist, philosopher, ethicist, artist, or man of religion, we are driven to consider the certitude of our knowledge. A friend of the writer's, when a student in a famous Eastern university, interrupted a professor with the comment: "That may be all right from our standpoint, but from God's point of view—." The student was interrupted in turn: "And *who* speaks from God's point of view?" Since, obviously, no one but God speaks from God's point of view, since no one knows as God knows, our task is to inquire how we may

---

3 Sayers, *Creed or Chaos?* *op. cit.,* pp. 28f.

seek to understand what God has seen fit to disclose. Various methods have been suggested.

There is the approach of the scientist: this includes the collection of data, examination and analysis, classification, testing of hypotheses, verification—in short, the empirical method. This scientific frame of reference is indispensable. The theologian, no less than the scientist, recognizes a dependable order in nature. The world operates with an observed, even a predictable, pattern. What the scientist refers to as "laws," the man of religion regards as God's providential plan. Neither the scientist nor the theologian is able to "prove" this orderliness; both observe and accept it. This is important not only for our understanding of the world itself, but also as an index to the moral and religious foundation of human life. The theologian is unable, after noting the dependable regularity of the natural order, then to believe that there is caprice or chaos in the realm of the moral and spiritual. The God of the atom and the God of the altar is the same God. The scientist may regard nature as "the way things are," but the theologian claims that they are this way because God ordained them so to be.

Of course, from a practical viewpoint the scientific way of thinking affects us every day. It provides detergents for our dishes and sudsy soap for our bath. It develops more "porky" pigs to replace scrawny razorbacks. It balances the generator on the airplane and enables the specialist to locate a jittery gall bladder—and remove it. It has successfully challenged the evil of poliomyelitis and promises the conquest of cancer. Among the "human sciences" phenomenal advances have been made in correcting personality maladjustments and in ministering to the dislocations in family and community life. It would be impossible to imagine the ruin in human life and institutions if the benefits of our scientific age were suddenly destroyed.

But is science adequate for all situations? The answer must be an unqualified "No." Science cannot provide an adequate motivation to guide us in right attitudes toward people of

other races. It can offer no standard for moral values to the
psychologically readjusted person nor put him in touch with
spiritual reality beyond the level of the human. Nor can it
interpret a Bach chorale. It is even unable to arrange flowers
on the table. I should hesitate to say with Nels F. S. Ferré that
there are thirteen ways the scientific method may lead us astray,
yet I am sure if we do not go beyond this method, our most
insistent questions about life will remain unanswered. We need
to be reminded that not only are the crucial questions of life
not *answered* by science; they are not even *asked*. "Science itself
is incapable of making moral judgments and it is not really too
wild a step of the imagination to think of a situation where
scientific knowledge is valued more highly than human lives." [4]

Again *the approach of the philosopher is important:* the
emphasis here is upon reason, logical consistency, coherence,
as Plotinus said—to help us to know "What matters most."
The theologian's debt to the philosopher is enormous. Tertul-
lian may deny that Jerusalem has anything to do with Athens,
but few concur in his judgment. When the proclaimers of the
Gospel were met by pagan thinkers they were compelled to
interpret the faith in the thought-patterns of a non-Christian
culture. The result was inevitable: Christian philosophy. Just
as both scientist and theologian accept the observed uniformity
of the physical order, so the philosopher and the theologian
recognize the need for clarity of thought in the intellectual
order. We say, "He is talking nonsense," or "He doesn't know
the facts," to emphasize the imperative for clear thinking as
well as moral action. We may not disown the solid academic
contributions of such men as Augustine, Anselm, Aquinas,
Calvin, and hundreds of less known persons. They struggled
to make ideas express the truth of God. And though in our
time representatives of Neo-Orthodoxy and Christian Existen-

---

[4] J. B. Phillips, *God Our Contemporary* (New York: The Macmillan Company, 1960), p. 28.

tialism may tend to repudiate rational metaphysics as adequate to interpret the Gospel, even Kierkegaard and Barth are intelligible only in proportion as they appeal to the sane judgments of their readers.

But again philosophy is not adequate for the most crucial issues of life. Reason alone is unable to explain the instinct of the mother bear as she protects her cubs. It cannot tell why a man would go to great trouble to aid an injured dog, or even more, to risk his life to rescue an enemy on the battlefield. It cannot account for the "reason" why Socrates was determined to drink the hemlock, and it speaks no word of comfort to a man on his knees in prayer. A philosopher once said: "I think that the most reasonable thing is to avoid having too much confidence in Reason." [5] Yet the theologian is persuaded that there *is* something beyond philosophy which may not be ignored. He concurs with Paul: "We even fight to capture every thought until it acknowledges the authority of Christ." (II Corinthians 10:5)

Nor can the ethical concern be ignored: in his search for truth man's moral sense has been insistent. Whether in Aristotle's endeavor to find the basis of a good society, or in the emerging struggle for justice in the work of the United Nations, the demand for the right cannot be overlooked. The only alternative to law and justice, for the individual or the social order, is sheer moral anarchy. A look at a small segment of history may seem to reflect success in a policy of exploitation, but the witness of the ages is that "righteousness exalteth a nation; but sin is a reproach to any people." (Proverbs 14:34, KJV) The moral imperative asserts that only the right is destined to survive; evil carries within itself the infection of decay. Thus the ethicist, as the theologian, claims that there is a moral foundation for human history just as there is a dependable structure in the physical order.

---

[5] Dixon, *The Human Situation, op. cit.,* p. 57.

It is when we move from *what* to do to the question of *why* it should be done that problems arise. How prone we are to think if we could only know the right, to get together a correct set of rules, to pass proper laws—then we would know and practice the truth. But there is frustration in our ethical concern. Painfully we learn that to know the right does not insure the doing of it. Trueblood reminds us that "we have inherited precious ethical convictions that seem to us to be profound, central, and essential." He then says: "But they have a curious inefficacy. *They are noble, but they are impotent."* [6] Any group of high school students can think up neat regulations for conduct without the slightest intention of putting them into practice. We have all felt a kinship with the little girl who said: "Why should I ask God to help me be good when I want to be naughty?" The moralist may call attention to the insistent category of oughtness, but ethics alone cannot account for the presence of this demand in human life. For the basic issue, after all, is not *what* is right—but *who* can do what is right. We must move beyond the question: "What is the moral demand?" We must ask: "What is the character of the person who is to perform it?" This is the theological question.

Then there are those who would turn to art as a path to truth: one of the most stimulating aspects of current religion is the theological interest in art. While definitive studies are yet to be written, there is a growing feeling that the character of man's spiritual life is often expressed more adequately in art forms than in rational analysis. Music, painting, drama, poetry, perhaps even architecture, may depict the human struggle in symbols more vivid, possibly more valid, than can be done by the use of words alone. The concern here is made to the sense of appreciation, of inner meaning and harmony, or on the other hand, to strife, tragedy, and the pain of existence,

---

[6] D. Elton Trueblood, *The Predicament of Modern Man* (New York: Harper & Brothers, 1944), p. 51.

until life is not simply written *about,* but intensely enacted. This is not a recent discovery. Interpreters have long recognized that one need not be an expert critic to see truth in a painting by Raphael or the frescoes of Michelangelo. Handel possesses the secret of singing a message of God into the soul even of the untrained person. Dante declares the truth of the Gospel in moving poetic drama. And the Cathedral of Chartres may be regarded as an architectural portrayal of the redemptive deed of God. Somehow there is a persistent conviction that beauty instead of ugliness, harmony rather than discord, goodness and truth and not evil and error, constitute the true nature of things. It may be said that the noblest achievements of any people are often seen in their artistic productions. And it is interesting to note that the ancient Hebrews, whose artistic skills were decidedly limited, expressed their creative genius entirely in their religion.

Roger Hazelton has discussed the relation of theology to art. He would argue that theology must not dismiss esthetics as irrelevant, since theology is to religious faith what esthetics is to art. That is, theology is not a substitute for art, but rather a corrective. Hence theology itself becomes an art when true to its own genius, since it, as other arts, uses symbols to convey truth. "Our Christian faith is never communicated except by means of symbols." [7] The most meaningful symbol, of course, is the Cross—used extensively by both theologian and artist. The Cross is the most universal symbol of the Christian faith, yet it is at the same time most inadequate. For it always points beyond itself to that which it seeks to reveal. When it becomes an end in itself, it ceases to be a symbol and becomes an idol. Thus Hazelton, following a suggestion of Tillich, regards all symbols as broken symbols, since they succeed in pointing to the reality beyond themselves only as they fail to claim ultimate

[7] Roger Hazelton, *New Accents in Contemporary Theology* (New York: Harper & Brothers, 1960), pp. 16f.

meaning within themselves. There is, therefore, at present a "massive search for images which can body forth old truth in new shapes and names," and this search "is already in full swing in architecture, drama, painting, music, and sculpture." [8] Hazelton's conclusion is most significant: "A theologian may aspire to think God's thoughts after him; an artist by the power of creative imagination is enabled to do God's work after him." [9]

While there is a measure of validity in the artistic approach to truth, this path is not entirely adequate. Someone has remarked that it is impossible to say an unkind thing in music. But when we hear some noises falsely masquerading under the name of music, it provokes us to say unkind things. Though it may appeal to some people, I confess the hideous pile of red and yellow bricks which comprises Keble College, Oxford, creates ugly discords in my own soul. It seems painfully out of place in an otherwise beautiful university city. And we must go beyond poetry. For example, the poems of John Donne express voluptuous license or the Christian faith, depending upon whether they come from the period prior to Donne's conversion or afterwards. I am persuaded that the way of art is nearer to life than is that of the scientist, the philosopher, or even the moralist. But art without the conscience afforded by religion can defraud and disgrace us. It cannot sit in judgment upon my sin nor offer absolution when I repent. In short, it offers no Risen Redeemer who has been involved in my broken sinfulness. With all the excellences of the current concern for art as an approach to Christian truth, still it stops short of the revelation of Jesus Christ as Lord.

Thus we must seek a more adequate method to answer the question, "How do we know?" From science one is led to say: "I experiment and discover." Through philosophy reason helps

---

[8] *Ibid.,* p. 31.
[9] *Ibid.,* p. 32.

me to conclude: "This is true." In the ethical concern I feel the imperative sense of moral oughtness. By means of art I am led to appreciate and enjoy. But it is when the insights of religion grip my total person I say: "I believe," "I respond," "I surrender." A century ago the religion of humanity proposed by August Comte was in vogue. Religion as he knew it was consigned to the childhood of the race, then was outmoded by philosophy as identified with the awkward adolescence of youth. But the true insight into the history of man was to be in the age of science, the positivistic adulthood of the race. Now the process seems inverted: we have utilized the resources of science and philosophy, but we live by hope that there is still the religious dimension in human life. We are driven back to religion to speak to the deepest needs of all.

It is as we come to religion that we inevitably encounter theology. For theology is merely the attempt to think clearly and communicate intelligently about religion. What proposals may be suggested, therefore, for the role of theology?

THEOLOGY AS DEFINITION

It was Whitehead who once spoke of the "fallacy of the perfect dictionary." We want religious truth arranged in neat little bundles, tied together in the symmetrical phrases of precise definition, like synonyms in a dictionary. Of course, theology as definition is not alien to the Bible. At least in four places theology as definition seems relevant to the Biblical revelation: First, in Exodus 3:14f the "Name" of Yahweh is stated: "I am who I am," or as Martin Buber has suggested, "I shall be present as I shall be present." It is true, this is not strictly a dictionary definition of God; it may not be regarded even as a completely adequate theological declaration of the character of God. But it does define the function, or activity, of God in relation to His creation. God is not at man's disposal; He can never be used by man to further human ambitions. At the same time God "will never be absent nor remote from Israel." He is henceforth to be reckoned within every historical situation.[10] Second, the Decalogue may be seen as a definition of the responsibility of man before God. These Ten Commandments occupy a unique position among the Hebrew people, since they possess the authority of a direct revelation of God. They "define" the covenant relation of God and man. Third, the Logos concept, described by Bouquet as "the Self-Expression of Ultimate Divinity," is possibly the clearest New Testament illustration of theology as definition.[11] Finally, the relation of God's action in creation to His action in redemption, requires theological definition. It is safe to assume that any adequate treatment of the subject will need to give careful attention to Biblical exegesis.

Likewise, in the history of the Church, theology as definition has had abundant expression. The *Summa Theologica* by Thomas Aquinas, regarded by the Scholastics as an "Introduction" to theology, may be suggested. But Protestant thought is not exempt from excessive reliance upon idolatrous concepts instead of living truth. The Scottish poet, Edwin Muir, expressed the memory of his theological boyhood in these lines:

> The Word made flesh here is made word again,
> A word made word in flourish and arrogant crook.
> See there King Calvin and his iron pen,
> And God three angry letters in a book,
> And there the logical hook
> On which the Mystery is impaled and bent
> Into an ideological instrument.[12]

---

10 Gerald H. Anderson, Editor, *The Theology of the Christian Mission* (New York: McGraw-Hill Book Co., Inc., 1961), p. 34.

11 *Ibid.*, p. 183.

12 See: *Expository Times* (July, 1959), p. 309.

It is one thing to give a dictionary definition, but this may easily fail to penetrate into the meaning of a situation. What, for example, does E=MC² mean? Yes, it is a formula for atomic fission. But does this really define the meaning? Suppose, for example, were to ask Tanimoto about E=MC². He might take us to a darkened spot on some seared concrete steps—the only remains of what was once a person, possibly his wife. No definition could interpret that! As Hodgson has said:

> We see things upside down and go hunting a will-o'-the-wisp when we seek to find reality by way of *analysis* instead of looking for it in the context of personal relationships.[13]

THEOLOGY AS PARABLE

There is also theology as parable. Stanley R. Hopper, Dean of The Graduate School at Drew University, commenting upon contemporary theology, says: "Theology today is confronted by the issue between theology of definition and theology of parable. Heresy consists not in statements which deviate from definition. It consists in passing by on the other side." [14]

Theology as parable more truly portrays life than theology as definition. Take, for example, the conference of the trees in the Old Testament. (Judges 9:7ff) When the trees desired a king, the olive tree, the fig tree, the vine in turn refused the honor, only to have the lowly briar, the bramble, the thorn, the thistle, accept the crown. The coronation speech of the scratchy bramble invited all the trees of the forest: "Come, and shelter under *my* shadow." (Judges 9:15, Moffatt) The parable is

---

13 Hodgson, *For Faith and Freedom,* vol. ii, *op. cit.,* p. 160. [Italics mine]

14 Stanley R. Hopper, "Methodism and the Current Theological Scene," *The Drew Gateway* (Winter, 1958), p. 118.

clear: when noble men refuse their vocation, it serves them right to be ruled by incompetents. Of course, it was Jesus of Nazareth who gave to the parable a permanent significance for the Christian faith. He took a truth, wrapped it in the garment of a story, and let it speak for itself, assuming that those who had ears to hear would hear. The true parable possesses the power of self-authentication. The story itself is its message since it speaks to the basic structure of human life lived under the grace of God. Take, for example, the parable of the man on the Road to Jericho. This has done more to interpret compassion, the healing of love which crosses all boundaries, racial and cultural, than all the systematic theologies from St. Augustine to Paul Tillich.

But this parable itself discloses the inadequacy of theology as parable precisely in what it does not say. Why was the man alone—on such a dangerous road? Did he have no friends on a dark night? Or is the aloneness a symbol of the "dark night of the soul"? Why were the official representatives of religion so unmoved by tragedy? Had they perverted the most profound perspectives of the faith they had inherited? Did their failure exhibit the fact that "the proper time" had come for God to act in a new way? And what of the man who beat up the victim? What happened to him? Was he a victim of his own crime, like Cain, a vagabond or fugitive from among his fellows? You see, Jesus died for him also. This is the theological issue. For the Gospel is not only concerned with the injured man on the Jericho Road, but with the man who put him there, with those who left him there, and with those who permitted the road to become infested with robbers in the first place.

Professor Joseph Sittler has discussed the literary device of the story as conveying affirmations about God and man and nature. In this medium is seen "the massive and organic story of man, man in his analysis and his anguish, his vision and his

dread, his lusts, longings, loves, and loneliness." [15] The theological issue is seen in the total context of this story enacted on
the Jericho Road: all the characters, both identified and implied, are involved in a community under the grace of God.
The parable excellently pinpoints one inescapable truth. But
the "massive and organic story of man" is bigger than this
truth. Theology as parable can be just what it is designed to
be, only a parable, a story. And as an illustration it may fail
to illustrate. There were in Jesus' day those who had ears to
hear but who failed to hear. Not always did even those who
lived in closest fellowship with Our Lord grasp the truth of
parable.

THEOLOGY AS DRAMA

May we then speak of theology as drama? Whereas theology
as parable is a brief story used to illustrate a truth, drama
weaves a plot sufficient to help me see myself exposed, un-
covered, unbuttoned, a living example of sin and salvation. In
a sense the Bible may be called "The Drama of Deliverance,"
with God's role as righteous redeemer of history climaxed in
the Lordship of Jesus Christ. It is not merely in the deliberately
constructed drama, Job, but in the total Biblical record that
this dramatic account of man's responsibility before God
and God's search for man is seen. Again and again dramatists
have gone to the Holy Scriptures to find enduring examples
of pathos, tragedy, humor, victory, in short, all the fundamental
themes of human existence. The Passion Narratives early in
the Christian era constituted the central theme of the Holy
Drama. The following dialogue between the angels and the

---

[15] Joseph Sittler, "The Context of Confirmation," in *The Christian Scholar*
(Winter, 1960), p. 301.

women at the sepulcher became a part of the liturgy of the church:

> Quem quaeritis in sepulchro, o Christicolae?
> Jesum Nazarenum crucifixum, o caelicolae.
> Non est hic, surrexit sicut praedixerat.
> Ite, nuntiate quia surrexit de sepulchro.*

Miracle plays and mystery plays, based upon Bible stories or portraying Biblical incidents, provided religious instruction not only for people unable to read but they did so in a manner designed to etch the scenes indelibly upon the minds of the spectators. The morality play, while not taken directly from the Bible, served to supplement the ethical instruction of the Scriptures by portraying the conflict between good and evil. And the poetic dramas of Dante and Milton would have been impossible were it not for the Biblical story.

The current interest in drama suggests its use to reflect the religious mood. Consider, for example, *J. B.,* or *The Dark at the Top of the Stairs.* Centuries ago the Greeks employed what they referred to as *catharsis.* As the spectator (note, the *spectator*) witnessed the conflicts within his own soul exposed to life on the stage—by vicarious identification with the actors he experienced a catharsis, a cleansing of the inner life, at least a release from himself and his troubles. I suspect something similar to this happens in the Roman Mass or in the Lord's Supper in the Protestant Church. It was Clement of Alexandria who spoke of Christ as "assuming the character of man, and fashioning Himself in flesh, He enacted the drama of human salvation." [16] Theology as drama, or drama

---

* Whom seek ye in the sepulcher, O Christians?
  Jesus of Nazareth who was crucified, O Heavenly ones.
  He is not here; he is risen as he foretold.
  Go and make known that he has risen from the sepulcher!

16 Clement of Alexandria, *Exhortation to the Heathen,* Chapter x.

as expressing theological meaning, has taken on a new significance. Roger Hazelton shows how one may, through drama,
identify himself as a Christian with the lives of people who
are haunted by the silent, absent God. He refers, for example,
to Samuel Beckett's *Waiting for Godot* and Albert Camus'
The Fall as raising theological issues "which may well make
God appear more real as an object of radical doubt than he
can ever be as the object of so-called faith." Hazelton then
says: "At least these works succeed in avoiding the downright
blasphemy which lurks within our conventional churchly piety,
the terrible profanity involved in taking God too much for
granted." [17]

Finally, a line from Langston Hughes fixes in dramatic form
the disillusionment, and the faith struggling to be born, among
the disinherited of the earth:

> What happens to a dream deferred?
> Does it dry up
> Like a raisin in the sun?
> Or fester like a sore—
> And then run?
> Does it stink like rotten meat?
> Or crust and sugar over—
> Like a syrupy sweet?
> Maybe it just sags
> Like a heavy load:
> Or does it explode? [18]

But again, theology as drama accents the role of those who
perform. A friend saw Othello from the box seat. He was able
to see the anticlimax of the tragic lovers, back of the curtain,
rise from their deathbed and walk away! They would do it
again the next night. The drama is done before us; it is per-

---

[17] Roger Hazelton, *op. cit.,* p. 30.
[18] Langston Hughes, *Montage of a Dream Deferred* (New York: 1951), p. 71.

formed for us. But it is not necessary for us to become a part of it. Catharsis may not happen. It is possible to sit through a two-hankie movie and go home merely emotionally "pooped." One may even hear the Halleluiah Chorus as only another musical number. And it is sadly possible to kneel at the altar of God to receive the Holy Communion with less commitment than eating a doughnut at a coffee break!

The deficient element in drama is lack of involvement. It can easily be something we witness rather than a segment of life in which we participate. The Biblical sense of drama accents the "happenedness" of the events. Neither God nor man could be spectators. There are no spectators in the drama where God has the chief role. Perhaps we should say drama lacks the crucial element of history. *Heilsgeschichte,* understood as "holy history," or "salvation history," emphasizes not only the mighty redemptive acts of God but also the involvement of men in their use or abuse of freedom. History, therefore, understood from within the theological context, includes more than some special kind of "faith-event" concerned either with the assertion of God's activity or only the meaning of the events for me. The tendency today to see the mighty acts of God as remembered events within the community of believers gives a new appreciation to the meaning of history. In a sense the present is even more than a memory of the past, the past is embodied in the present. In this way, therefore, we are delivered from simply a mythological view of the past. We are delivered from an agnostic view of the past. We are delivered from thinking of the past only as something completed once and for all. The past as contemporary with the present is involved in a Christian philosophy of history since every believer participates in the redemptive acts of God in living in the community of faith, the church. But this, of course, goes far beyond drama. It is more than drama which is true to life. It is the drama which is life.

THEOLOGY AS ENCOUNTER

Must we, after all, turn to theology as Encounter? The Existentialist says: "All real living is meeting." [19] If I understand him, he is saying: to be alive is to encounter others, The Other. This can become a morbid thing, as in Sartre. He writes *No Exit*, a one-act play in Hell—set up as a drawing room, perhaps symbolic of the 20th century. One man and two women are sentenced for crimes against humanity (The proportion may be a bit out of balance!):

Garcin: Alone, none of us can save himself or herself;
   we're linked together inextricably.

As they discuss their plight, they learn that together they cannot save themselves—all they can do is talk and torment each other.

Garcin: So this is hell. I'd never have believed it.
   You remember all we were told about the torture-
   chambers, the fire and brimstone . . . Old Wives'
   tales! There's no need for red-hot pokers.
   Hell is—other people! [20]

But there is another perspective. "Meeting," "Encounter," may be seen through the eyes of Christ: "As he looked at the vast crowds he was deeply moved with pity for them, for they were as bewildered and miserable as a flock of sheep with no shepherd." (Matthew 9:36) "For wherever two or three people

---

[19] Martin Buber, *I and Thou* (New York: Charles Scribner's Sons, 1958), pp. 11, 34.

[20] Reprinted from No Exit and The Flies by Jean-Paul Sartre as translated by Stuart Gilbert, by permission of Alfred A. Knopf, Inc. Copyright 1946 by Stuart Gilbert, pp. 38, 61.

come together in my name, I am there, right among them!"
(Matthew 18:20)

Some years ago Emil Brunner put into a small book the
line: "The Biblical conception of truth is: truth as encounter." [21] On the deepest level of life truth is personal, the
meeting with others, especially with The Other. It is communication in terms of a meeting which defies definition,
which transcends parable, which is drama but drama having
become incarnate in human experience. This communication,
this Encounter comes in vivid, at times, in horrifying ways. An
auto wreck reveals a mass of twisted steel which was once a
car. We look at it and suddenly there is a deeper dimension
as the slow drip, drip, drip of blood spatters below it. A quiet
room in a library becomes different—when the soft footsteps
of another are heard. When Robinson Crusoe saw a footprint,
all the world of his island was different. A friend, visiting Mos-
cow, went to church. When a Russian woman learned that she
went, not as an inquisitive American tourist, but as one to
worship, the Russian woman burst into tears and through an
interpreter said: "You're not just a tourist; you stayed the
whole time. You came to worship God!"

This is Encounter. This is Theology as Encounter. This is
truth mediated in a manner far beyond any verbal symbols.
Theologically, every moment I walk the razor edge of the
abyss. Every hour, every decision, is fraught with eternal significance. Every moment is a moment lived out before God.
Every moment is eschatological. This is the example that "all
real living is meeting."

THEOLOGY OF THE KERYGMA

Martin Luther was right: there is no way from man to God;
there is only the way from God to man. This is the truth of

---

[21] Emil Brunner, *The Divine-Human Encounter*, translated by Amandus W.
Loos (London: SCM Press Ltd., 1944), Foreword, p. 7.

the Incarnation. "God was in Christ personally reconciling the world to Himself." (II Corinthians 5:19) This was God's way of participating in the brokenness of human life. He slipped into human history almost unnoticed and looked out on the distorted human scene. There He saw the anxiety, the woe, the death, through human eyes. Until, may we dare to say it, even God Encountered the meaning of human existence—as even God had never known it before: in human experience! This has been so vividly presented by J. B. Phillips that his complete statement seems to require its quotation:

> The Christian religion asserts that nearly two thousand years ago God, whose vast and complex wisdom science is daily uncovering, visited this small planet of ours in Person. Naturally the only way in which he could do this was by becoming a human being, and this is precisely what Christians believe that he did. This is the heart and center of the Christian Faith, this is the Gospel or Good News which those who had witnessed this extraordinary event went out to tell the then known world. That God so inserted himself into the stream of human history, and that we are consequently living on a visited planet, are statements audacious enough to take the breath away, and no reasonable person could be expected to accept such a belief as fact without considerable thought and careful examination of the evidence. To have had God, reduced to the stature of a human being, but indubitably God playing a part in the earthly scene, is a staggering thought. But this is where Christianity starts, this is the rock on which it is founded, and this is the point where men are compelled by the nature of the event to make up their minds as to whether it is true or false.[22]

I am indebted to J. Oliver Nelson for this story. In a university in India, without a single Christian student, the program was to dramatize the great religious leaders of the world. With imagination the students entered into the experience. Buddha was portrayed under the Bo tree. Mohammed set out on a pilgrimage to Mecca. Confucius sat with the *Analects*.

---

[22] Phillips, *op. cit.*, p. 52.

Various deities of the Indian pantheon were represented. Then, one lad took a rough purple robe and laid a crude crown of thorns on his head—and stood in the middle of the stage. The audience, *without a single Christian in it,* sat in shocked silence. Then someone hissed, and another, until a chorus of objections drove the lad from the stage. I heard Oliver Nelson then say: "There is one figure of religion, the Bloody-headed Carpenter of Nazareth, who couldn't be lampooned!"

This is Theology as Encounter. This is theology as kerygma. This is the Gospel which created the Christian Church. In a theology of definition, the Word becomes word. In a theology of parable, the word becomes story. In a theology of drama, the word becomes a role. But in a theology of Encounter, "The Word becomes Flesh!" In a theology of definition there is analysis. In a theology of parable there is analogy. In a theology of drama there is action. But in a theology of Encounter, there is acquiescence. It is this surrender which enables one today to proclaim the kerygma. "In the beginning was the kerygma."

Simon's Soliloquy

I was coming in from the fields that day
When I met the mob, moving on its way
Toward Calvary. I paused to see the One
Who stumbled, struggled, yet staggered on
Beneath His cruel load, the mark of shame.
And then above the noise I heard my name:
"Simon, foreign dog, bend low thine arm
And lift the thing from off this fainting form!"
I stooped to lift—and then I stopped to stare:
For, oh, the Form was One I'd met before!
That day when I was sore beset by pain,
He came and touched, and I was well again.
His voice was such that all my fears had fled;
My heart felt pure—"Thy sins are gone," He said.
Long as I live I'll ne'er forget that look
Of pain yet peace—though not a word He spoke.
And in my soul there crept a sense of power—
A mystic warmth—unlike I'd felt before.

My body too, seemed strong—invaded there
By courage, pity, and a resolve to share
His load. I bent and gripped the heavy thing,
And as we walked my heart began to sing—
"Is this a cross? I thought 'twas hard to bear,
But now it seems that life anew is here
Within my breast, and joy complete, divine"—
And then I knew—it came so clear—I saw—
I was not bearing His cross:
He was bearing mine."

The Parson

Index

Index

BIBLICAL INDEX